BOOKS BY JUDITH HERBST

Sky Above and Worlds Beyond
Bio Amazing

BIO AMAZING:
A Casebook of Unsolved Human Mysteries

BIO AMAZING:
A Casebook of Unsolved Human Mysteries

by JUDITH HERBST

ATHENEUM • NEW YORK

Chapter 10 contains excerpts from pages 20, 43-45, 51-53
of *RECOLLECTIONS OF DEATH: A Medical Investigation*
by Michael S. Sabom. Copyright © 1982 by Michael B. Sabom.
Reprinted by permission of Harper & Row, Publishers, Inc.
and from *LIFE AT DEATH* by Kenneth Ring,
copyright © 1980 by Kenneth Ring.
Reprinted by permission of The Putnam Publishing Group.

Library of Congress Cataloging in Publication Data

Herbst, Judith.
   Bio-amazing.

   Bibliography: p. 140.
   Includes index.
   SUMMARY: Explores such unexplained human phenomena
as hypnosis, spontaneous human combustion,
and extrasensory perception.
   1. Human biology—Miscellanea—Juvenile literature.
[1. Human biology—Miscellanea] I. Title.
QP37.H47   1985   612   85-7446
ISBN 0-689-31151-6

Atheneum
Macmillan Publishing Company
866 Third Avenue, New York, NY 10022
Collier Macmillan Canada, Inc.
Printed in the United States of America
Published simultaneously in Canada by
Collier Macmillan Canada, Inc.
Type set by Heritage Printers, Inc.,
Charlotte, North Carolina
Printed and bound by Fairfield Graphics,
Fairfield, Pennsylvania
Designed by Marilyn Marcus
10   9   8   7   6   5   4   3   2

For you, Dad

with love and respect

Contents

BIO AMAZING:
A Casebook of
Unsolved Human
Mysteries

The Strange Case of the Identical Twins

"There are more things in heaven and earth, Horatio, than are dreamt of in your philosophy."
—HAMLET

On a midwinter night when the skies are dark and clear, you can see two heavenly brothers shining high above you. They are the stars Castor and Pollux, named after the identical twins of Greek mythology. According to the tale, when Castor was killed, Pollux was so overcome by grief, he begged the great god Zeus to let him die so he could join his brother. But Zeus, normally willing to oblige such requests, had never before seen such a powerful relationship. Greatly moved by Pollux's devotion, Zeus decided instead to bring

3

Castor back to life. Then, to insure that the twins would remain together through eternity, he gave them immortality and placed them side by side in the sky.

Identical twins do indeed have an unusual relationship, more unusual than most of us realize. Their bond is not only an emotional one, but during those few critical days following conception, it is also a physical one.

All of us begin life as a single fertilized cell, practically invisible, but packed with a tremendous amount of genetic information. Every detail is there: our eye and hair color, the shape of our nose, the very pattern in which our cells will grow to form skin and muscles, bones and tendons. Within twenty-four hours the cell makes a copy of itself, and the magic of growth has begun.

The cell divides to form two cells, attached like movie tickets. These two cells then become four; the four become eight; the eight become sixteen, and so on until there is a little ball of cells ready to start folding and shaping itself into the embryo that will soon be a human being. But three times in every thousand births, that early group of cells breaks in half. The two cell groups continue dividing and growing independently, and from a single fertilized egg cell come two people—identical twins. So for the first forty-eight or seventy-two hours of their life, identical twins are literally one human being.

This is most dramatically illustrated by so-called

Siamese twins who, through an error in cell division, never completely separate in the womb. It may be a mere two cells that remain attached, but as development continues, the link becomes more extensive, and the twins may be born joined side by side at the shoulders, the pelvis, or, on extremely rare occasions, at the head. Siamese twins usually share limbs and sometimes organs, often making the job of separating them difficult or impossible. When a separation can be attempted, success becomes, in a way, a matter of opinion. The twins are clearly part of each other, and the operation, while considered corrective surgery by the rest of us, is actually an amputation. Shortly after separation, Siamese twins have often been observed to become extremely lethargic and depressed. They move around very little in their crib, spend a great deal of time sleeping, and do not display the emotions and activities of normal infants.

When Siamese twins are born joined at the torso with two separate and perfectly formed heads, we naturally assume they are two individuals. They each have, after all, their own brain. The brains function independently, but the body they share cannot. This unusual situation poses a very interesting question: How many people are there? One? Two? Perhaps one and a half?

Although they are not physically joined at birth, identical twins once were contained within the same cellular mass. How much of that early connection remains beyond the moment of bodily separation? And could this short-term link be the clue to the following mysteries?

"This is one of those cases in which the imagination is baffled by the facts."

—WINSTON CHURCHILL

The scene is a classroom during the New York State Regents Exam in English. Identical twins Ruth and Nancy Schneider are working hard on their compositions. They have each selected a subject from the several choices given in the test. Their ballpoint pens fly across the blue-lined paper, carefully crafting an essay that will be worth a large percentage of their grade.

The clock ticks on, and at last Ruth and Nancy finish their tests. They hand in their papers and leave together. The urge to talk about the exam is overwhelming. Every student has it. "How did you do on the grammar section? What did you write your essay about?" But with Ruth and Nancy there is no need for discussion. Unknown to each other, Ruth and Nancy have written *nearly identical compositions*. They chose the same subject and developed it in the same way. Their words, their phrases, their sentence structure are almost perfect matches.

Did they cheat? Of course not. Because of the nature of the assignment, they could not possibly have prepared their composition in advance. First of all, the only thing you can bring into an English Regents is a pen. Second, there is simply no way to anticipate what kinds of topics the Board of Regents will come up with. The subjects could be anything from "The Conquest of Mexico" to "Candlelight Memories." This makes the Regents essay something of a surprise, requiring fast footwork and improvisation.

It's even more ridiculous to suggest that Ruth and Nancy copied from each other during the test. One reason is the logistics problem. How, in the space of an hour or so and under the watchful eyes of a proctor, could a person copy, word for word, no less than two pages of running script? Furthermore, handing in duplicate compositions would have spelled nothing but trouble for Ruth and Nancy. It would most certainly have indicated that they had cheated, and the penalty would have been a failing grade. Nobody in their right mind would take such a chance.

So there's not much left to offer as an explanation except the obvious. The Schneider twins, quite independently, were thinking and doing the same thing at the same time. Their brains were synchronized, their thoughts in perfect rhythm, identical right down to the commas and periods.

One person or two?

Going back to the year 1955, we have John and James Cramp who are sitting back to back with crayons and pieces of paper in front of them. They are asked to draw a picture. A short time later, the twins inform everyone, at the exact same moment, that they are finished. The pictures are placed side by side. The twins giggle knowingly. The drawings they have made are identical.

"Curiousier and curiousier!"

—ALICE IN WONDERLAND

Mary Brooks has gone in for surgery while her identical twin sister, Selina Strong, paces anxiously in the hospital waiting room. All at once, Selina is overcome by chills. A shape forms before her eyes. It is Mary.

"Liny," whispers the vision. "I'm leaving now."

Selina panics. "No!" she shouts. "No, Mary! Don't go! I'm coming!"

The time is 2:30.

But Selina doesn't go to Mary because she can't. Her twin lies on a hard operating table beneath a thin paper sheet, under a stainless steel blade that cuts and draws blood. Mary is far beyond Selina's reach. Or is she?

When the surgery is over, Selina is told that Mary is fine. The doctor is smiling, but then he remembers. "It all went well," he says, "except for the part where that sister of yours gave us quite a scare."

"What happened?" Selina cries, but she already knows.

"Mary went into cardiac arrest," replies the doctor, "at about two thirty."

What are we to make of Selina's vision and apparent knowledge that Mary was near death? Was Mary somehow "communicating" with her twin?

It is not at all unusual for twins to literally feel each other's pain or know, without being told, when their twin is ill or suffering in some way.

On November 13, 1958, at 12:15 in the afternoon, Kenneth Main suddenly experiences chest pains. Four days later he is again wracked with pain, and this time seeks medical help. A physical exam, however, shows nothing out of the ordinary, and Main is told he is in perfect health.

Meanwhile, unknown to Main, his twin brother Keith lies in a hospital while surgical stitches are removed from his chest. Four days earlier Keith had undergone an operation to repair a hole in his heart. The first incision was made at 12:15.

When Barbara Morgan began having morning sickness and backaches, she immediately telephoned her twin sister Gillian.

"What's wrong with you, Gillian?" she asked. "I don't feel very well."

Curious? Indeed it is. Gillian, as it happened, was pregnant, making her the *second* person to learn the news. Her twin was the first.

Several months later, on the twenty-sixth of March, Barbara went into labor, but it was Gillian who gave birth. Even stranger, when Gillian was injected with pain medication prior to delivery, Barbara dropped off to sleep.

Twin telepathy? Let us explore further.

"... and in death they were not divided ..."
—THE BIBLE

An airplane is down! In an instant it has been crushed beyond recognition, turned into a mass of roaring flames. Somewhere else, a woman stops what she is doing. Her entire body seems to be on fire. The phantom heat engulfs her. She staggers to the floor, terrified, writhing in pain. Then, all at once, the heat is fading, fading away, and a great black void sweeps over her.

Now an emergency crew is speeding to the crash site. Rescuers are pulling charred bodies from the wreckage. Later, when the grim task of identifying the bodies has begun, they will find the woman's twin sister among the dead.

Did this woman actually share her twin's death agony? Did she, for a few monents, "die" in the plane crash, too? Or was her twin somehow communicating her very last experience on Earth?

It may be said that the two major events in our life are birth and death. Since identical twins share not only their birth, but their very conception, wouldn't it be in the realm of possibility that they can also share their death?

"When you have eliminated the impossible, what
ever remains, *however improbable*, must be the
truth."

—SHERLOCK HOLMES

Most identical twins seem to be able to read each
other's thoughts. They can communicate feelings and
ideas by eye contact alone. Words, they claim, are
often unnecessary. During conversations, one twin
usually knows what the other is going to say and will
sometimes finish his or her sentences. Many of us have
occasionally done this with a family member or a close
friend, but with identical twins it is a far more frequent
phenomenon.

In the laboratory, scientists have recorded the brain
waves of identical twins, and the results are astonishing. The twins' wave patterns are almost exactly alike.
Their sleep cycles also match. The dreams of identical
twins last very nearly the same amount of time and occur with the same frequency and at the same intervals—
every eighty-five minutes, for example. But even more
amazing, identical twins often have very similar
dreams. One pair of twins reported a recurring childhood dream about an elderly woman who lived nearby.
Both dreams were frightening, and the endings were
identical.

Perhaps identical twins engage in a powerful kind
of mental telepathy. Without even being aware of it,
they are able to send messages back and forth, rather
like a combination transmitter/receiver. The transmit-

ter sends out signals along a certain wavelength, and the receiver, already preset to that wavelength, picks up those signals.

Albert Einstein, one of the most brilliant physicists who ever lived, believed that mental telepathy is a very real phenomenon. He even worked out a formula to describe it in mathematical terms. Einstein said that the intensity of the signal grows proportionately weaker as the distance between the sender and receiver increases. This, incidentally, is exactly what happens to radio waves. Of course, Einstein's belief in telepathy does not mean the phenomenon is a reality. However, if anybody can be considered the best candidates for it, it would surely have to be identical twins whose brain waves are so remarkably similar.

> "We'll use a signal I have tried and found far-reaching and easy to yell. Waa-hoo!"
>
> —ZANE GREY

Years ago, when identical twins were put up for adoption, they were sometimes separated and given to different families. If the adoption occurred early enough, the children would never know they had an identical twin. Usually, the adoptive parents didn't know it either. Recently, though, Dr. Thomas Bouchard of the University of Minnesota has been tracking down these separated twins and reuniting them. Not surprisingly, in nearly all the cases, the twins' reaction is indescribable joy but, more significantly, the twins also express a feeling of relief. One man said he had always thought there was something missing in his life, that he wasn't quite a complete person. When he saw his brother for the first time, it was truly a reunion, a "joining again."

Of course, Dr. Bouchard's twins showed the expected similarities. They looked alike, sounded alike, and scored within a few points of each other on intelligence tests—all of which Bouchard had anticipated. But there was something else, a whole string of weird coincidences that nobody could really explain.

Bridget and Dorothy had strangely given their children almost exactly the same names. Their sons are Richard Andrew and Andrew Richard. Their daughters are Catherine Louise and Karen Louise. And Bridget adds, "I had intended to name my daughter Catherine, but I changed it to Karen at the request of a relative."

Both twins, it was learned, had owned cats named Tiger, wear the same perfume, and like to read historical novels, written, amazingly enough, by the same author! But even more bizarre is the coincidence of the diaries. Both women kept a diary, same color, same style, for only one year—1960, and the entries, although different in content, were made on the exact same days.

Barbara and Daphne also like books by the same author, and at one time they had dyed their hair the exact same shade of brown. Both met their husbands at a town hall dance and were married in the fall. When they were fifteen, both had fallen down a flight of stairs and both now have weak ankles as a result of the accident.

Although Jake and Keith had never been told they were twins, Keith says he had somehow always known he had a brother, and Jake claims he always wanted one. When Bouchard brought them together, they slipped easily into a kind of brotherly comedy routine that was so smooth, it suggested something they had taken years to perfect. As with all the other twins in the study, Jake and Keith were kept apart until after their interviews, but every night they called each other on the phone. Once in the lobby of their hotel, they entered adjacent phone booths and simultaneously dialed each other's room number.

Jake and Keith, says Bouchard, are the most nearly identical twins he has ever seen, and yet, curiously, Jake is left-handed and Keith is right-handed. When asked to draw a picture of a house for one of the tests, Jake put the door on the left, and Keith put it on the right. In all other respects, though, the houses were almost exactly alike.

Helen and Ethel had met briefly for the first time when they were very young. Both showed up wearing the same dress, but even more astonishing, Helen had borrowed the dress from a friend!

When Jack and Oscar met, they both had moustaches and were wearing wire-rimmed glasses and two-pocket blue shirts with epaulets. Both brothers read magazines from back to front, and when they remove a rubber band from something, they automatically put it on their wrist.

But absolutely nothing can compare to this oddball set of coincidences:

For openers, both twins were named Jim by their adoptive parents. Jim and Jim married and then divorced Linda and Linda. Then they married Betty and Betty. Their step-brothers are Larry and Larry, and their sons are James Allen and James Alan. Each Jim had a dog named Toy.

All clear so far?

Jim and Jim drive a Chevy and a Chevy. Jim was a sheriff's deputy and Jim was a sheriff's deputy. Both Jims gained the same amount of weight at the exact same time and spent one of their vacations in Florida along the same three-mile stretch of beach. They smoke the same brand of cigarettes, drink the same brand of beer, and are the only ones on their block to have a tree in their yard with a bench around it.

Is this the result of thought projection? If the answer is yes, how do we explain all those similar names? In the Jim case particularly, the men certainly didn't chose their wives based on their names. They surely had no say in their step-brothers' names, not to mention their own. And as far as children's names are concerned, the choice is generally made by both parents together. Furthermore, neither twin knew the other one even existed!

What is this extraordinary bond between identical

twins? It seems to transcend time and distance, joining them spiritually and emotionally to one another in a way that leaves the rest of us baffled, and curious, and maybe a little envious. What must it be like to almost feel another person's heart throb, know his or her thoughts and feelings, stand without and yet be within? Indeed, it is a mystery of life itself. It is nothing short of bio amazing.

"It worries you, this case?"
"Naturally it worries me. I cannot make head or tail of it."

—AGATHA CHRISTIE

CHAPTER 2

The Supersense Mystery

Mrs. J. is awakened in the middle of the night by a particularly disturbing dream. She nudges her husband who lies softly snoring beside her.

"Arnie!"

Her husband stirs. "Whazzat!"

"Arnie! Don't fly to Boston tomorrow! Take the train. Please! Cash in your ticket and take the train!"

Arnie J. rolls over. "Train? Boston?" He rubs his eyes and blinks.

Mrs. J. is now sitting up, beads of perspiration gathering on her forehead. "I saw it! The plane had engine trouble. It was . . . just falling . . . like a stone. . . ." She shakes her husband. "Don't take the plane, Arnie!"

Mrs. J.'s husband nods sleepily. "I'll take a different flight," he mumbles. "OK?"

Mrs. J. breathes deeply. "Yes," she whispers. "Another flight."

The following morning, Arnie J. turns in his ticket for Flight 302 to Boston. He isn't quite sure why, but he does it anyway. Forty-nine minutes later, Flight 302 develops engine trouble and crashes just outside of Baltimore. Arnie J. calls his wife from Boston and tells her he'll be home in time for dinner.

A B C D ESP

ESP, as almost everyone knows, stands for extrasensory perception. It's the so-called sixth sense, the one that comes after sight, hearing, taste, touch, and smell. ESP allows us to lift objects just by thinking "Up!" read other people's minds, know what's inside sealed envelopes without looking, and predict the future. ESP is a supersense, all right, and if science can prove that people actually have it, then physics and human biology are going to need some very heavy rewriting.

ESP certainly deserves points for stamina, because for years it's had to fight to be accepted. "Real" scientists didn't take it seriously, and any time one of them started dabbling in ESP, he or she immediately became the bad kid on the block. Today, though, the list of ESP researchers includes esteemed men and women from major universities. They conduct their experiments according to the strict rules of the scientific method and have published their results in some of science's most respected journals. Recently, Dr. Paul Sargent broke the ESP prejudice barrier when he became the first person to receive a PhD in parapsychology from England's Cambridge University. Maybe the laughter and snide remarks haven't completely disappeared, but at least they're not as loud as they used to be.

Although thousands of people claim to have ESP, the ability has always been extremely hard to measure under laboratory conditions. For instance, a woman insists she has psychokinesis. She says she can move objects without touching them, but in the lab she can't even affect the roll of dice. The number she is thinking of turns up slightly more often than pure chance would dictate. Then there's the researcher in the Midwest who gets good results with one of her experiments, but when parapsychologists on the West Coast try the experiment, they fail to duplicate the work. Why? What goes wrong?

Dr. Sargent believes the problem lies in the nature of ESP itself. It's like a talent, he says. Some people have it, some don't. Furthermore, when ESP is present, it's usually very weak. Nobody goes around levitating couches or automobiles. A psychokinetic person apparently has to use a tremendous amount of effort just to slide a paper clip across a table top. While some psychics contend they can see several years, even decades into the future, the greatest number of correct predictions are those made only hours or days in advance. ESP's weakness may be due to the fact that it is not yet fully developed. Perhaps the ability is just beginning to evolve.

According to Darwin's theory, evolution has changed us in hundreds of ways over the years. We are still being shaped and molded, made better and more efficient with time. ESP could be a future sense, one that we will need to meet the universe hundreds of centuries from now. Telepathy, teleportation (thought travel), and psychokinesis may be necessary when we move out towards the stars.

One of the biggest criticisms of ESP research concerns the test conditions. Skeptics feel the subjects may be using their "normal" senses to pick up subtle clues. Without realizing it, the experimenters may also be cluing the subjects with body language—a swallow, a muscle twitch, a bead of perspiration. Eyes may be the worst culprits of all. Our pupils respond not only to light, but to emotions as well. Anger, enthusiasm, fear, and hopefulness dilate and constrict the pupils. Experimenters who root for their subjects to do well may unknowingly be giving away the answers, and the subjects may unknowingly be interpreting these answers.

So, to pinpoint ESP, to really zero in on it, we have to get rid of as many senses as possible.

Dr. Sargent thinks he has found the solution. First, he blocks out the subject's hearing with white noise. White noise is a steady stream of nonsense sound, like radio static. Sargent eliminates vision by placing Ping-Pong ball halves directly over the subject's eyes.

Virtually blind and deaf, the person lies motionless in a little cubicle and waits to receive information via extrasensory perception. Actually, this technique serves a double purpose, according to Sargent. With information streaming through our five senses, ESP messages are almost completely drowned out. When subjects are in sensory isolation, they can more easily focus in on themselves and hear the faint broadcast coming through the ESP network.

The minutes pass, and the subject, whom we shall call Phoebe, gets more and more in touch with herself. She notices the rhythm of her breathing and feels her heart beating. Thoughts come and go, and come and go, like waves lapping against a shore. This is the ESP readiness phase. Phoebe's mind is being prepared to receive images. On the average, the readiness phase takes about twenty minutes.

Meanwhile, in another room, a picture is selected to be sent out over WESP, your station for clairvoyance. An assistant concentrates on the picture for several minutes while Phoebe tries to pick up the image. Finally, Phoebe is shown the target picture and three other distractor pictures and asked to select the one that came into her mind during the sender phase of the test. If Phoebe picks the target picture, she scores a *hit*.

Now, the odds are one in four that Phoebe will choose the target picture. That is, she has a twenty-five percent chance of scoring a hit. If Phoebe correctly selects the target picture once, it means nothing because the hit can be attributed to chance. But suppose Phoebe goes through five of these tests. Each time the pictures are different. The more hits Phoebe scores, the longer the odds get. The chances of her scoring two hits in five tries are smaller than if she scored one hit in five. They're even smaller if she hits three out of five. In fact, three out of five is such a long shot, it suggests that something other than chance is operating here. Phoebe may very well have ESP.

Most people probably figure if Phoebe has ESP, she ought to be able to identify all the target pictures. But if ESP is really a weak sense, if it has not yet fully evolved, then five out of five is asking a lot. It's like demanding that someone with a hearing impairment listen for the sound of a pin dropping. The person does indeed hear, but not so acutely.

Paul Sargent's research looks promising. His subjects are doing better than chance, and their scores improve with time. It is almost as if they are teaching themselves to be more receptive. But the real test will come when independent researchers can achieve similar results with Sargent's technique.

Pick a Card, Any Card

Surely you know this one. A magician fans out a deck of cards and invites you to "Pick a card, any card at all. Don't show it to me," he says and hides his eyes.

You display the card—the five of diamonds—to the audience and then slip it back into the deck.

Shuffle, shuffle, shuffle.

The magician taps the top of the deck. "This one," he says and flips over the first card. Presto! The five of diamonds.

That's a magic trick, of course, performed by sleight of hand. No matter what it looks like, no matter how astonishing and mysterious it seems, it is not clairvoyance. These are the cards used to test clairvoyance.

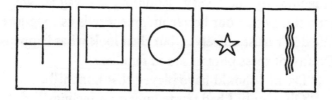

Clairvoyance is one kind of ESP. The word literally means "clear sight," and it describes the ability to perceive things without getting help from any of the five senses. Paul Sargent is testing clairvoyance when he asks his subjects to identify the target picture from a group of four. The ESP deck is a variation.

The experimenter deals twenty cards face up behind a screen or in another room. The subject is then given a fresh pack of ESP cards and asked to match the symbols on the twenty hidden target cards. Five hits out of twenty is chance. If you randomly selected twenty cards from the deck and laid them out, you would probably match five target cards.* Eight hits in

_____

* You have no doubt played the card game "War," that endless battle between two armies of cards. You and your opponent

twenty starts to look suspicious. More than ten is very suspicious and suggests that the subject knows what's on the cards. It could indicate clairvoyance.

It is, in fact, entirely possible that all of us are clairvoyant to some extent. Consider, if you will, that common phenomenon known as the hunch. There probably isn't a person alive who hasn't had a hunch, a sneaking suspicion, a funny feeling about something. Hunches, by their very definition, are vague, wispy little things that our better judgment tells us to ignore. We don't trust ourselves, but then look what happens. Do any of these phrases sound familiar?

"Darn! I should have played that hunch!"

"Oh, if only I had trusted my own feelings!"

"I knew it! I JUST KNEW IT!"

Then there are what can be called the super hunches. A super hunch is a powerful sensation that demands attention simply because it is so strong. It strikes a handful of people maybe once in an entire lifetime, so it really cannot be classified as clairvoyant ability, but it does seem to be a true clairvoyant message. For a moment in time, the person somehow tunes into radio station WESP (or KESP if you're on the West Coast) and suddenly receives a news bulletin.

An American soldier found the right frequency

---

each turn over a card from your pack, and the highest card wins. If you turn over the same card, it's war. Turning over the same card is random matching and bound to happen every now and then which is why the game is playable.

during World War II. He was alone in a foxhole when all at once he was seized with the knowledge that he had to get out of there. The feeling was so clear, so urgent, so unmistakable, that the soldier never hesitated. He bellied his way out of the foxhole and was perhaps twenty yards away when he saw a flare scream into the foxhole and strike it dead center.

A young woman recalls her father leaving the table after dinner one night to take a leisurely stroll around their farm. He had been gone only a short time when the woman was overcome with a terrible fear. She knew something had happened to her father. He was in danger somewhere, somewhere among all that vast acreage or perhaps beyond.

The woman ran across the land searching the fields, the thousand and one nooks and crannies, the buildings and storage bins, but there was no sign of her father. She checked with neighbors, but no one had seen him. Several hours later, the woman's father returned with the following story.

He had been walking in the nearby woods when he came across an old barn. Drawn by the mystery that all deserted buildings have, he entered and started to look around. He was inspecting some old, rusty tools when all at once he heard the unmistakable clicks of a rattlesnake. The snake was huge and only a few feet away, coiled and ready to strike. Despite his almost paralyzing fear, the woman's father managed to grab a wooden plank and beat the snake to death.

Although the young woman had not known what

the danger was, she was certain that it existed. No questions, no doubts, no second thoughts. She knew.

From powerful feelings we go to concrete images. A young college student tells of a sudden clairvoyant episode involving a missing woman, the wife of one of the faculty members. The student had never met the woman and didn't even know what she looked like, but for weeks after the disappearance, the student had the same vision over and over again.

The body of a woman was lying in a puddle of icy water in a swampy, wooded area. The student could see that the woman was wearing a hat and that her coat had a fur-trimmed collar. She could not pinpoint the location, but she said there was a road that cut across the main highway not far from the college. She kept getting the impression of turning left onto the road.

It was a woodsman who finally discovered the body nearly two months later. He had turned *left off the main road*. In a dismal, *swampy area*, he spotted the lifeless form clad in a *hat and coat with a fur-trimmed collar*. The body was lying *in a puddle of water*.

Apparently, this student had never before displayed clairvoyant ability. How or why she had tuned in at this particular time is certainly a mystery, but it suggests that ESP may be available to all of us—if the conditions are right.

In the 1970s, a dramatic experiment was carried out at the Stanford Research Institute in California. The subject was former police commissioner Pat Price, a man whose clairvoyant abilities were astonishing, to say the least. To this day, science is still baffled by Price's performance.

Picture, if you will, a small, quiet cubicle deep within a laboratory for the investigation of psychic phenomena. Pat Price settles back into a comfortable chair, calm and confident. Physicist Russel Targ waits expectantly, fiddling with a tape recorder, imagining, perhaps, the man who is at that moment getting into a car five miles away. The man has told no one where he is going. He doesn't even know himself. His final destination will be the result of haphazard right turns, left turns, and U-turns; of spontaneous freeway entrances and exits. He has no idea where he will end up and neither does Pat Price, but when he does arrive, Price will know. Somehow, Price will know.

After a while Price closes his eyes. "What I'm seeing is a . . . boat dock," he says, "or a boat jetty. . . . Definitely, lots of little boats. Uh . . . motor launch . . . uh . . . sailboats. . . . Definitely, definitely, uh . . . boat dock or jetty."

Price is absolutely correct. The car has pulled into a marina. Sleek, expensive boats sit tranquilly moored in their berths, their colorful sails unfurled like butterfly wings. The afternoon sun glints off the water.

Price continues. His brow wrinkles. "It's funny . . . uh . . . something just flashed in . . . uh . . . Chinese or Japanese pagodalike effect."

Targ interrupts "Did that pagoda effect have anything to do with the boat dock that you saw initially? Is that near where they're standing?"

"Uh-huh. It's behind them. Uh . . . it's, uh . . . it's like a restaurant, highly manicured, long. . . ."

It is a restaurant, built in the shape of an Oriental pagoda.

That summer Pat Price took part in nine remote viewing tests, as Targ calls them, and described seven of the sites with astounding accuracy. Sometimes Price mentioned features that the driver of the car hadn't even noticed, and this convinced Targ that Price was not using telepathy. Instead, Price seemed to be seeing the sites from overhead. It was almost as though he were a helicopter pilot scanning the area until he spotted the driver of the car. Then he made his "descent." One of the locations was a swimming pool complex, and as Price drew the lay-out on a piece of paper, he included the dimensions of the pools. He was off by only ten percent.

Other researchers have conducted similar remote viewing experiments and achieved equally striking results. One man, almost two thousand miles from the target site described,

". . . circular patterns, and rings, and disks, as if looking down on them from the top. It looks like a large saucer, just sitting in the middle of a city . . ."

The target site was the Superdome in New Orleans.

What is the mystery of remote viewing, and how are these people doing it? There seems to be no identifiable sense organ, like the skin or the eyes, through which the information can be received. Is it possible that there is a sixth organ which we have yet to discover? Science, quite frankly, hasn't the faintest idea.

A Dream Come True

When we wish for our dreams to come true, we are really talking about what Webster defines as: "a strongly desired goal." At least, that's what the vast majority of us mean. But some people, it seems, have nighttime dreams that, hours later, become actual waking events.

Take the case of the woman who lost a piece of luggage while on her way to New York by train. Railroad personnel began the search but were unsuccessful in locating the trunk. One night, in her hotel, the woman had a dream in which she saw the snow-covered trunk sitting on a station platform. The baggage claim check was missing.

The following morning, the woman telephoned the railroad to report that she had "located" the trunk. She described her dream and was promptly met with the all-time biggest guffaw on record. Curiosity won out, though, and the company contacted each station all the way down the line. Sure enough, the trunk was found, snow-covered and ticketless, on one of the platforms.

This is remote viewing with a twist. The images came to the woman disguised as a dream. She was asleep, with all of her senses set on low. Unlike the person who exercises clairvoyant ability in the waking state, this woman did not have to concentrate deeply or focus all her attention on the incoming pictures. She did not have to contend with distractions from her other senses. The ESP channel was wider than ever. Sleep, then, may turn out to be the ideal condition for receiving information via ESP.

Some ESP dreams seem to be precognitive; that is, they give the dreamer a glimpse of something that will happen in the future. One man dreamed he had entered a horseroom (a room used for illegal off-track betting). In the dream, the man clearly saw the toteboard and an entry named Ringo's for the second race at Belmont. He bet ten dollars on Ringo's to win and woke up.

That morning, the man went out of town on business and, having arrived too early for his appointment, stopped at a luncheonette. While he was sipping a cup of coffee, the counterman casually mentioned that if he were interested, there was a horseroom in the back. Intrigued, the man entered the horseroom and sure enough, Ringo's was posted on the board for the second race at Belmont. The odds were twenty-to-one. It certainly would have been something if the man had bet according to his dream. Ten dollars would have returned two hundred. But the man didn't trust himself and just for fun bet a dollar to show (third place). Ringo's hung back through the entire race, made his move at the last minute, and crossed the finish line first.

* * *

The following dream is amazing for its length and richness of detail. As the actual events unfold, you can't help feeling that the man's entire life had already been written, like a book, and that in the dream, the man accidently read too far ahead.

A Precognitive Mystery in Two Acts

Act I—The Dream
The man is in a bus station on his way from Fayetteville, North Carolina, to Athens, Georgia, where he lives. He had been to visit his mother who had suddenly fallen ill. A young woman sitting nearby asks for his help in trying to get a call through to someone stationed at Fort Bragg. The man explains how to go about it, and when it comes time to board the bus for Athens, he notices that the woman is behind him in line. They sit together during the trip, and the woman tells him her name is Barbara Jackson and that she is from Macon. Before long, the man asks her for a date, and she accepts. Since the man has never been to Macon before, the woman thinks he might have trouble finding her house, so she suggests they meet in the lobby of the city's main hotel.

The scene shifts, and the man is now at the hotel. He inquires about a room for himself and is told there are no vacancies. He eventually winds up at the Sydney Lanier a few blocks away. While he is waiting for the girl in the hotel lobby, the man notices the photograph of a soldier hanging on the wall behind the registration desk. Later he learns that the soldier is a local boy who had been decorated during the war. The girl arrives, they return to her house, and the dream ends.

Act II—Real Life
The next day, the man receives word that his mother is ill, and he immediately heads for North Carolina. Not twenty-four hours after his dream, he is living the events right down to the smallest detail. He takes the bus from Fayetteville and meets a girl named Barbara Jackson. He asks her for a date, she accepts, and they arrange to meet in the lobby of a Macon hotel. The hotel has no vacancies, but the man finds a room at the Sydney Lanier. He notices the picture of a soldier hanging over the registration desk. Absolutely everything is just as he had dreamed it.

But wait just a minute, here. Sleep researchers have all pretty much agreed that dreams are creations of our own mind. We make them up using the raw material of our experiences. That's why people who are born blind don't dream in images. They can't. Images are not part of their experience. If you follow this line of thought, in a precognitive dream, a person must then be *making up* what will happen to him or her in the future. It would be like sitting down with a map and working out the exact route for a car trip from Seattle to Denver. You select every highway, every scenic overlook, every rest stop, restaurant, rest room, every gas station, every motel, and every tourist attraction.

The next day you jump in the car and head out according to plan.

Is it possible that we really have that much control over our life? Can we map out even the tiniest, most insignificant details? And what happens to all those people around us? They have plans, too. Can we affect their plans? Can they affect ours?

Whew! What a mess!

But on the other hand, let's assume we have no control. Let's assume precognitive dreams give us a glimpse of a future that has already been worked out—every success and every failure, the foods we will eat, the clothes we will buy, all our friends, the test grades we will get in school, the exact make and model of our first car. We simply act out a part that has been written for us, and we're not allowed to make any changes.

Now, although information about our future is available, it's hard to get at. A steady stream of todaynoise keeps roaring in through our five senses and drowning out the tomorrowdata. But when we're asleep, those senses are operating on low voltage. Sight is eliminated. Hearing, touch, taste, and smell downshift into first gear. We are in an altered state of consciousness, and the level of todaynoise falls dramatically.

Listen.

Can you hear it? Can you see the tomorrowdata images slipping in? Because we are asleep, we think it's a dream, but it's actually tomorrowdata, a peek at what will be.

But a theory is only as sound as the facts that support it, and the one fact we have about precognitive dreams is that they occur. Why some people are more sensitive than others, and how the information originates and is transmitted remains, to date, completely unexplained.

The Crystal Ball Connection

The fortune-teller has had a long and checkered history. In biblical times, fortune-tellers or seers, as they were called, were respected and rather awe-inspiring individuals. They may or may not have had genuine abilities, but their reputation was certainly much better than it is today. Today's fortune-teller is associated with big golden earrings, turbans, tent shows, and more showmanship than anything else. But while many fortune-tellers and self-proclaimed psychics are indeed frauds, a few people do seem to show precognitive ability in the waking state. They are fully conscious, all five senses blaring like the Air Force Marching Band. In precognitive circles, they are the top bananas. Unlike someone who has a once-in-a-lifetime precognitive dream, these pros can, in a sense, put in a request for their information. They don't have to wait for a delivery; they go out and get it. Even better, their range is enormous. They can predict what's going to happen to other people, to men and women they've never met.

Now, a lot of people make predictions. Take

weather forecasters, for instance. Weather forecasters use science to draw conclusions about the way certain conditions will affect our atmosphere. Physicists and mathematicians make predictions, too, and theirs are in the form of equations. Einstein's magic math predicted black holes, those weird, burned-out stars with the big appetites. Mathematics predicted the existence of Neptune and Pluto and what will happen to the sun in the far distant future.

Science fiction writers don't predict, exactly, but they do speculate. They use a dash of science and a dash of imagination to create a world of the future, and they happen to be amazingly good at foreseeing what will come to pass. Robots, lasers, space ships, test-tube babies, the jet pack used by the space shuttle astronauts, and a staggering amount of other present-day realities were all born in a typewriter.

But none of this is precognition. Psychics usually know very little about the subject matter of their predictions. They do not spend hour after hour poring over charts, diagrams, typewriters, and miles of computer print-outs. Psychics most often receive their knowledge about the future in the form of visions. You may think of the crystal ball as strictly cartoon fare, but many psychics still rely on it as the source of their precognitive visions.

Years ago, seers gazed into pools of water, ink, oil, mirrors—any reflective material that was available. Surely you remember how the wicked witch in *Snow White* kept trying to wheedle information out of her mirror. The crystal ball, however, is state of the art not only because it is a beautiful object, but perfectly formed crystal globes have always been hard to come by.

The crystal ball itself is not extraordinary; it's the psychic who's special. Whether the vision actually appears within the ball is debatable, but it is more likely that the psychic, while in a trance, receives mental images through ESP.

Psychic predictions that are very specific naturally carry more weight than those of a more general nature. Predicting a tough year for the President of the United States is hardly evidence for ESP. Every year is tough. Warning him of an assassination attempt, complete with time and place, is more like it.

Predicting the future is tricky stuff. Nobody is ever one hundred percent correct, but if ESP is really as weak as Dr. Paul Sargent believes, mistakes and failures are certainly understandable. It's hardly fair to scream, "Fraud!" if a psychic prediction is wrong. Instead, we ought to do some investigating when the prediction is right.

The following psychic predictions were all reasonably specific and certainly could not be attributed to educated guessing.

• On November 25, 1967, Joseph DeLouise predicted a bridge collapse. Less than a month later, the Silver Bridge spanning the Ohio River in West Virginia collapsed, killing forty-six people.

• In 1968, DeLouise said that two trains on the Illinois Central Railroad would be involved in a wreck in the Midwest. About a month later, the train wreck occurred—forty-five miles outside of Chicago on the Illinois Central line.

• DeLouise again. In May, 1969, he foresaw an airplane crash near Indianapolis. The number 330 would be very important, he said, but he didn't know quite why. DeLouise also predicted that seventy-nine people would be killed.

September 10, 1969, 3:30 P.M. An Allegheny Airlines jet collides with a private plane over Indianapolis. Four crew members and 79 passengers are killed.

• Famous psychic Jeane Dixon predicted that Robert Kennedy would be assassinated in California in 1968. He was.

• Irene Hughes foresaw the death of three men in a space ship. In 1967, a fire swept through Apollo I killing the three astronauts Virgil (Gus) Grissom, Edward White, and Roger Chaffee.

Perhaps even more intriguing are the cases in which the same prediction is made by different psychics. Assuming there was no "professional conspiracy," the following are rather extraordinary.

Criswell on television in March, 1963: John F. Kennedy will not run for reelection because something will happen to him in November.

Jeane Dixon in a magazine in 1952: A young Democrat will become president and will be assassinated during his term of office.

Irene Hughes in her diary: President Kennedy will be assassinated.

Bill Linn: John F. Kennedy will be killed.

In November, 1963, John F. Kennedy, Democratic President of the United States, was shot and killed by an assassin's bullet.

Joseph DeLouise in December, 1968: Tragedy for Senator Edward Kennedy. Water will be involved. A woman is going to drown.

Irene Hughes over a Canadian radio station in June, 1969: Ted Kennedy will be involved in an automobile accident near water. His passenger will be fatally injured.

On July 18, 1969, Ted Kennedy drove his car off a bridge and his companion, Mary Jo Kopechne, was drowned.

But to be objective, it should be noted that these same psychics and their colleagues have also made some very wild and crazy predictions.

David Bubar foresees spray-on invisibility. It will come in an aerosol can, like deodorant or oven cleaner, and when applied, will make us invisible. (Bubar may have been reading too much H. G. Wells, who proposed a similar idea in a dandy story called *The Invisible Man.*)

Criswell figured that in 1983 all the women in St. Louis would go bald. (Anybody who lives in St. Louis knows how that one turned out.)

Edgar Cayce, who died in 1945, said Atlantis would rise from the sea in 1968. A lot happened in 1968, but the magical appearance of Atlantis wasn't part of it.

Still, we are left with quite a few examples of precognition—not just from renowned psychics but from plain old folks, the kids next door. Apparently, some people are catching pieces of the future through a sense we have yet to identify.

In 1975, scientists at the Stanford Research Institute conducted a controlled experiment in precognition. The subject was asked to predict where one of the researchers would be in half an hour's time. The researcher, meanwhile, was far from the lab, driving around aimlessly in his car. On the front seat were nine sealed envelopes, each containing a card with a different destination. The researcher had no idea what was in the envelopes.

Sitting almost motionless with eyes closed, the subject said, "It's very dark, and at the end you come through an archway into a very bright area where there's lots of vegetation, like a rose garden. It's very formal. It's a very manicured kind of garden."

After the subject had finished her description, a computer randomly selected the driver's destination. It was given as a number that corresponded to one of the numbered envelopes. The computer chose location six, and for the first time, the researcher learned where he was to go: Stanford Hospital Plaza.

Thirty minutes after the subject had made her prediction, the researcher found himself passing under one of the arches that led into a beautiful courtyard. Fine, carefully tended shrubs and small bushes stood in straight rows, and the researcher was struck by the elegance of the garden. The morning sun glinted off the white concrete, and the researcher blinked, trying to adjust to the glare. The walkway he had just crossed had been bathed in shadows.

The psychic's precognitive description had been incredibly accurate. Somehow, this woman had seen an event that would not occur until half an hour later, and she had done it under strict laboratory conditions. The researchers were baffled and a little concerned. The laws of physics were wobbling. They did not allow for precognition. Suddenly, the accepted concept of time was being challenged. How could a person know about something that did not even exist? It began to look as if the future, the past, and the present all flowed into each other or, even worse, were one and the same!

You know, if you look at the sky on a clear, dark night you can see the past. Because light travels at a finite speed (186,000 miles per second), it takes time to reach us. Just like a train, light leaves the station and begins its journey. In two seconds, light has gone 372,000 miles; in four seconds, 744,000 miles. Light from the sun takes eight minutes to reach our eyes, so we are seeing the sun, not as it is now, but as it was eight minutes ago. The more distant the star, the further back in time we are able to see. And it's all because of physics. Physics allows us to view the past.

Might it also allow us to view the future?

Think about this for a minute:

If Madam Mosca the Magnificent sees an event from tomorrow in her crystal ball, does that mean the event has already occurred somewhen else? Or is she only seeing what might occur? Does she see the *potential* for an event?

A book resting on a table has potential energy. If it falls off the table, it uses this energy. It doesn't have to fall off the table. It may remain there for a hundred years or a thousand years, but as long as it does, it retains its potential energy.

Now, suppose Madam Mosca can detect the potential energy of an event. (The event is made up of billions of bits and pieces of matter, all with their own potential energy.) She says, "I see Horace Snodgrass slipping on a banana peel in front of the Astrodome." Of course, Madam Mosca doesn't want that to happen, so she gets a Houston phone book, looks up Snodgrass,

Horace, calls him, and warns him not to go to the baseball game. Then, just to make sure, she sends him two tickets to a Texas Rangers game. Since Horace likes freebies, he decides not to go to the Astrodome and doesn't slip on the banana peel.

Did Madam Mosca see the future? The answer is yes and no. She saw only the potential for one scenario. Science can measure an object's potential energy. Perhaps some people can detect the potential energy of an event.

Psychical research is gaining momentum, but we are still far, far away from the finish line where all will be revealed to us. Actually, this is not so bad. It keeps science moving ever forward in its quest to discover the deepest secrets of the human mind and body. And this, of course, reminds us that it is not the mystery that is bio amazing, but the detectives.

The Great Shut-Eye Mystery

The REM Song

Every night while you are sleeping,
Comes a motion slowly creeping,
And your eyes begin their sweeping
Left to right, and left to right;
Back and forth they go a-racing
With a tempo and a pacing,
So they look like they are tracing
Little movements in the night.

> *Chorus*
> *Right to left, and left to right,*
> *We will REM five times each night;*

To and fro, and fro and to,
I'll be REMming, so will you.

What a funny situation
Is this eyeball stimulation,
It exists for the duration
Of the dreams that you devise;
But your pupils never focus
On an image or a locus,
So, what is this hocus-pocus
Of your roly-poly eyes?

(*Chorus*)

Now, we know there is a section
That we'll call the Pons Connection,
In a down-and-out direction
Of the brain's amazing stem;
We have learned from brain wave tolling,
It's the pons that is controlling
All your eyeball rock and rolling,
So, we know the cause of REM.

(*Chorus*)

But, my goodness, what an action!
What an absolute distraction!
And we have no satisfaction
Since we still cannot explain
Why our eyeballs pitch and tumble,
Like an earthquake on the rumble;

Oh, it keeps us very humble,
Our sneaky little brain.

(Chorus)

So, tonight before you wander
To the land of dreams up yonder,
Take a little time to ponder
All the mysteries of dreams;
Though you think that sleep is dreary,
Just a time-out for the weary,
I've got news for you, my deary,
Sleep is wilder than it seems!

(Chorus)

In an average lifetime, you will spend upwards of twenty-five years sleeping. It won't be out of choice, but out of necessity, although no one knows quite why. Every sixteen hours or so, the release of various chemicals in your brain will force you to stop what you are doing and pay your prisoner's debt. And nearly every animal in the world will go right along with you, all members of the mysterious sleep chain gang, from the smallest rodent to the largest elephant. We understand very little about the sleep phenomenon and yet, ironically, it is as essential to us as breathing. Indeed, the evidence seems to suggest that if we don't sleep, we could very well die.

The ancient Greeks believed that sleep was a

temporary spell cast by the god Hypnus. Each night Hypnus flew around fanning people with his huge wings. Then, a short time later, his son Morpheus, the god of dreams, took over.

Other societies thought the soul left the body during sleep and went on a series of adventures. It was therefore considered quite dangerous to wake up a sleeping person. If the soul were caught off guard and not given enough time to reenter the body, the person would awaken without a soul and immediately die. The sleeper was just a shell, much like a dead body, and in one of Shakespeare's plays, *Hamlet*, the main character, does indeed consider the similarity of sleep and death. (Hamlet was pretty upset at the time and toying with the idea of doing himself in.) But Hamlet was hardly the first to think of sleep as a kind of pseudo-death. After all, for eight hours we really are oblivious to our surroundings. Consider the phrase, "dead to the world," which is often used to describe someone in a deep sleep. So it is not surprising that many children fear sleep, and the concept of the sandman, a gentle being who sprinkles eyes with magic sleep dust, was probably developed to convince them not to be afraid.

Through the years, literature has given us several notable sleep champs. In a short story by Washington Irving, Rip van Winkle nods out for twenty years. Sleeping Beauty goes nonstop for a hundred, and according to legend, King Arthur is not really dead, but sleeping. That would make Arthur the longest snoozer in history at about fourteen hundred years and still counting.

Although there is a great range in people's normal sleep periods, sleepathons like these are pure fiction. Some people insist they must get upwards of ten hours of sleep, while others need as little as four. There are even cases of people who seem to be able to condense their sleep and wake up feeling refreshed after a mere two hours. But despite the fact that our parents usually tell us we need eight hours, eight is only an average. A person's body knows instinctively how much sleep it needs, and when it has had enough, it will automatically rouse itself. You can sometimes force more sleep on yourself, but you certainly can't challenge Rip van Winkle. Conversely, you can also force yourself to stay awake for a few hours past your normal bedtime, but again, the body sets strict limits. It will put up with only a short extension—say, nine or ten hours—and if you try to postpone sleep for much longer than that, you will find your sleep center taking over and practically conking you on the head.

"Enough is enough," it seems to be saying. "You've had your fun, but now out you go."

Apparently, this bullying on the part of our sleep center is for our own good. The truth is, if we go without sleep for too long, some very strange things begin to happen, as New York disc jockey Peter Tripp proved in 1959.

Tripp staged a "radiothon" to raise money for the

polio fund. His intention was to do his regular three-hour evening show and then remain awake continuously off the air for as long as he could. To encourage donations to the fund, he moved from the broadcasting studio to a glass Armed Services recruiting booth in the middle of Times Square. He had a suite of rooms in a hotel across the street where he washed up, changed his clothes, and ate his meals. A staff of physicians and scientists monitored Tripp's health and administered batteries of tests to measure attention span, reaction time, and so forth.

The first twenty-four hours went fine. The public flocked to the recruiting booth, mostly out of curiosity, and saw a professional radio announcer doing his stuff without the slightest problem. The monsters, however, were waiting in the wings.

Tripp hit his first major snag after about two days. He began to hallucinate. He had been about to change his shoes when he suddenly dropped the one he was holding because he saw cobwebs inside it. Later, in the broadcast booth, Tripp said there were bugs all over the table, and he demanded to know who had put the rabbit in the corner. Meanwhile, his test performance was dropping. The slightest thing broke his concentration, and he had to summon all of his willpower to get it back. He was spending more and more time on each question and not always coming up with the right answer. He had grown nervous and fidgety.

By day five Tripp's hallucinations had taken on a whole new dimension. They were expanding in size and scope, becoming much more threatening. Tripp saw a scientist's tie squriming and jumping around as though it were alive. He recoiled in horror from one of the nurses who he said was leering at him and dripping saliva. A psychiatrist's tweed suit looked to him like a blanket of furry worms. That evening he ran screaming from his hotel room because he thought flames were shooting out of the bureau drawers. He had grown suspicious of everyone and accused the medical staff of plotting against him. Tripp was in bad shape. Continual wakefulness was taking its toll.

Day six—almost one hundred forty hours without sleep, and Tripp was now disoriented. He didn't know where he was or even who he was. He kept staring at a large wall clock in the broadcast booth, imagining it was the face of an actor he knew made up to look like Dracula. After a while, he couldn't tell if he were Peter Tripp or the disembodied Dracula face. The doctors and nurses seemed more menacing than ever. Tripp was convinced they were out to get him, planning something awful, and he had to be constantly reassured.

But what is perhaps the most amazing part of Tripp's ordeal is that the listening public had absolutely no clue that anything was wrong. For a few hours each night, Tripp did his show with astonishing self-control. He played records, read commercials, announced the time, did weather forecasts, chatted with the audience— all without a single blooper, flub, or embarrassing remark. He didn't even sound tired! Tripp seemed to be holding a small section of his mind in reserve. Even though he was actually displaying signs of severe mental illness (paranoia and hallucinations), he was somehow able to override them when he had to.

Tripp's terrifying journey through his sleep-starved mind finally ended on the tenth day. Just prior to his last broadcast, Tripp suffered a grotesque hallucination involving a neurologist who had come to examine him. The doctor asked Tripp to lie down, and as he was bending over him, Tripp's paranoia suddenly emerged full-blown. He imagined that the doctor was an undertaker sent by the medical team to bury him alive. Seized by sheer panic, Tripp bolted from the room, screaming hysterically. His eyes were wide and glassy, his heart thundering in his chest. He fought off everyone who tried to contain him. To see him like that, no one would have ever believed him capable of speaking coherently, let alone doing a three-hour radio show for hundreds of thousands of people. But that evening, Tripp was behind the microphone as usual, carrying off what can only be called a bio amazing feat. Then, after one last physical exam and a run-through of the test questions, Tripp let the sandman carry out his assigned orders.

Obviously, something very important had begun to break down inside the body of Peter Tripp. The doctors couldn't detect any physical changes, but there is no doubt that Tripp's mind was short circuiting.

Up to now, it has been assumed that sleep is a little like stopping off at a service station to fill your car with gas. Sleep restores us, revitalizes us, allows our body to replace whatever it is that we use up while we are awake. But while the theory appears to make sense, there are problems with it. First, not everybody needs the same amount of sleep. Second, in many animals, sleep time and waking time seem to be all out of whack. Elephants stomp around the savannah for about twenty-two hours, leaving only two hours to restore themselves through sleep. The oppossum is just the opposite. What could it possibly be doing during its six hours of wakefulness that it requires eighteen hours of sleep to counterbalance? Oppossums do not lead such hectic lives! And then there are the shrews—a kind of rodent—and some types of fish, which may not even sleep at all!

It has been suggested that sleep may be ridding our body of certain chemicals that build up during the day. If we don't sleep, these mystery chemicals will reach toxic proportions and could eventually kill us. The theory is certainly interesting, but so far, no one has identified these chemicals or explained how sleep might be getting the job done. Nevertheless, whatever sleep is or does, the process is incredibly effective. Disc jockey Peter Tripp was able to repair his eight sleepless nights' worth of damage in just thirteen hours.

We do know that sleep is a general slowing down of bodily functions. Breathing, heart rate, blood pressure, and body temperature all decrease. For approximately eight hours, you are neither hungry nor thirsty. Your sense of sight has been temporarily eliminated. Your sense of taste, touch, smell, and hearing are dulled. You are aware of your immediate environment, but your awareness is limited and selective. You are curiously able to ignore the familiar, such as a clock ticking or traffic sounds, but will often respond to something sudden and unfamiliar—a thunderstorm, for example, or a cold draft in the room.

Scientists have peeked at sleep with a spyglass called an electroencephalograph, or EEG for short. The EEG is a machine that records brain wave patterns, and when we go to sleep, we leave very distinct tracks. Our brain waves change quite dramatically; but they do not match the brain waves of an unconscious person or someone in a coma. Sleep, then, is a unique state, quite different from anything else.

It's awfully boring to watch somebody else sleep, but the scientists and the EEG have discovered that it isn't boring at all to be asleep. Sleep is a roller coaster ride, up and down, and up and down through four levels, or stages, all night long. Stage I is the level closest to consciousness and the level from which it is the easiest to rouse someone. Stages II through IV take you deeper and deeper into the mysterious Land of Nod. You spend about forty minutes in Stage IV and then begin your ascent back to Stage I, making five round trips each night. Every time you hit another level, your brain waves change, which is, of course, how scientists discovered the four levels of sleep.

Without a doubt, dreaming is the weirdest part of sleep. It occurs almost exclusively in Stage II, and we all do it, whether we are aware of it or not. For some, dreams appear in technicolor, while other people claim they only dream in black and white or grays. Blind people dream just like everybody else, but the form their dreams take depends on when they lost their sight. People who have been blind since birth dream in sounds and textures, while people whose blindness occurred later in life continue to dream in pictures. This suggests that we draw on our experiences and memories to fashion our dreams. That makes us the writer, producer, and director of our dreams. We usually have a starring role and absolute say in who acts out the other parts. We supply the props and the costumes. Five times a night we are creative geniuses without even trying.

Midnight at the Movies Presents
DREAMS
Astounding . . . Baffling . . . Unexplained
Filmed on location with a cast of thousands
Five Shows Nightly

You have been asleep for perhaps an hour. Your muscles are relaxed. Your chest rises and falls with the slow, even rhythm of your breathing. There is a calm, almost angelic expression on your face. Silence and peace surround you. The clock on your dresser ticks out the minutes to showtime. Four . . . three . . . two . . . one . . .

And suddenly the curtain is up! Your eyes are roll-

ing back and forth, back and forth, back and forth behind your closed lids. This is it! This is REM, the
amazing, mysterious Rapid Eye Movement that signals
a dream is in progress. You appear to be watching
something, but your eyes are not looking at anything
at all, because blind people also display REM.

REM begins quite early in our development as human beings. It seems to be controlled by a part of the
brain called the pons, which is located in the brain
stem. Research has shown that as soon as the brain stem
develops in the fetus, there are signs of REM. So it
looks as though we all start dreaming even before we're
born, but what fetal dreams are like is anybody's guess.

. . . back and forth, back and forth, back and
forth . . .

This is the dance of REM. Somewhere deep inside
your mind you are creating a little drama for an audience of one. Your story, though, can hardly be called
one of the year's ten best. It's almost impossible to follow. The events are confusing and disconnected. The
characters come and go for no apparent reason. The
dialogue doesn't make any sense. It's a mess, all right,
but you don't seem to notice it. On and on you dream,
accepting even the most ridiculous situations without
question, thoroughly convinced that it's all really happening. Furthermore, you are not just a sleepy member
of the audience; you're a participant, and you react to
everything that goes on. A frightening dream in particular catches you like a hook, and you actually experience fear.

OHMYGOSH!
*You're in the back seat of a speeding car and there's
no driver! You try desperately to reach the steering
wheel, but you can't move. Crazily, the car swerves
off the road. The brake! You've got to reach the
brake!*

Meanwhile, back in your bedroom, your heart is
thundering. Your breath is coming in quick, shallow
bursts. Beads of perspiration break out, soaking your
pajamas and pasting your hair to your forehead. Your
blood pressure has shot up, and the adrenalin is pumping, pumping, pumping.

*Suddenly the car is on a high cliff. The speedometer
needle is climbing ... 90 ... 100 ... 110 ... You can
see the edge of the cliff just ahead. It's an endless
drop to nowhere. Do something! DO SOME-
THING!*

Your terror in this dream is very real. You are not
pretending to be scared; you *are* scared, and all the
readouts in the sleep laboratories prove it. The readouts
also show something else. You are almost completely
paralyzed. With a few exceptions, your muscles have
lost so much tone, they are literally immoveable. We
do indeed toss and turn and roll around quite a bit while
we're sleeping but not during a dream. During a dream
we have about as much ability to get up and walk
around as our pillow does. Scientists believe the pur-

pose of this strange paralysis is to prevent us from acting out our dreams.

Although sleepwalkers appear to be giving a dream performance, they are not. In fact, sleepwalkers are in an entirely different level of sleep. They are sound asleep but strangely mobile. No one knows why some people—several million in North America alone—sleepwalk. This bizarre activity may begin at any time in a person's life and without any apparent cause. Sleepwalkers are completely unaware of what they are doing and usually remain ignorant unless they are told about it. And even then, they will strenuously deny it. They'll insist they've been asleep all night, as, of course, they have. But while they've been snoozing upright, they have been involved in some very strange activities.

Like fleshy robots, they will suddenly open their eyes, swing their legs over the side of the bed, and head off on some mysterious midnight errand. Talk to them and they won't answer. Wiggle your fingers in front of their eyes and they won't see you. They will, however, steer their way around furniture, take the dog for a walk, do their grocery shopping, and even drive a car.

But sleepwalking is only funny in the cartoons. Scores of people have been injured during a walk because they managed to climb out onto window ledges thinking they were stepping onto their front porch. Members of the family have been taken for intruders and attacked. It is a ridiculous myth that if you awaken a sleepwalker he or she will get lockjaw, die of a heart attack, or become paralyzed. The danger, instead, lies in what the sleepwalker is doing, since these people have been known to get themselves into some pretty scary situations. Unfortunately, sleepwalking is as mysterious as dreaming, and science has not yet come up with a way to prevent a person from going on midnight strolls.

Of course, sleepwalkers dream, just like everybody else, which makes for a pretty active night. They return to bed, settle in, and slip easily into the next level of sleep. Before long, they are involved in more excitement, but this time their muscles are holding them prisoner. Now they have to be content to stay put while a whole series of strange events unfolds before them.

Sleep researcher Stephen La Berge has identified something about our dreams that most of us experience but few of us are aware of. La Berge calls the phenomenon "lucid dreams." A lucid dream is one which you recognize as a dream. You almost say to yourself, "Hey! Hold on, here. This is a dream. All this stuff is fake. I'm dreaming!"

La Berge believes that once we know we are dreaming, we have the ability to control the outcome of the dream on a conscious level. We can change whatever we don't like. He says he has learned to alter his dreams while he's asleep, and he can teach others to do the same. But if dreams, as they unfold naturally, are important in some way, perhaps we shouldn't be fiddling with them. Perhaps we should let nature take its course. Who knows? Maybe dreams are serving a very definite purpose, whether we remember them or not.

Dreams seem to be speeded-up versions of events, like a movie run in fast forward, but actually, dream-time parallels realtime quite closely. If it takes you three seconds to open a door in realtime, that's how long it will take you to open a door in your dream. The speed at which you do things in a dream is only an illusion, because you edit the scene. If you begin to walk across a bridge in your dream, each step will match your waking steps, but you get to the other side faster than normal because you have edited out most of the steps. They are not necessary to the plot, so to speak. That's why you are able to be in a wheat field one minute and standing on a street corner the next. You simply eliminate the travel time for the sake of the "real" action.

You are also able to put your dream into slow motion. You can slow down an attacking tiger to keep him from grabbing you. If you're running through deep snow, you can slow down the steps to make the event very frustrating. Why you do this, however, is unclear, although it may have to do with the purpose of the dream itself.

In our lifetime we will crank out 125,000 dreams. No one knows why. Sigmund Freud, the father of psychoanalysis, thought that dreams were a way of releasing our deepest desires and needs, the ones that society frowns upon or the ones that we, for some reason, won't let ourselves express. If you remember your dreams, then you probably know that they are either very scary (the things we are afraid of), or bold and daring (our hidden desires), or unbelievably frustrating. There are dreams in which we leap tall buildings in a single bound, try desperately to catch buses that keep eluding us, and run for our lives from horrible monsters. Freud felt that all these dreams were speaking in symbols to us. He said they are a way of telling ourselves about ourselves, of rummaging around in our brain attic to see what's in there and maybe straighten up a bit. According to Freud's theory, the more a person is concerned about him- or herself, the easier it is to remember the dream. But to get anywhere with a dream, you first have to figure out what all the symbols mean. Water, to Freud, represented birth, a man represented your father, railroad tracks were a death symbol, and so on.

Freud made great inroads in the study of the mind, but his dream theory seems to have fallen out of favor with many dream researchers. Most scientists today admit that dreams are far more complex bits of mind stuff than we ever, well . . . than we ever dreamed. Nature has provided us with a truly bio amazing mechanism. Now, if we could just figure out what it's for. . . .

The Hypnosis Mystery

There used to be a time when the highlight of a cocktail party was the comedy performance given by one of the guests with the help of an amateur hypnotist. Amateur hypnotists were always invited to little gatherings along with Harry-from-the-office who could play the piano. It made for a well-rounded evening. Hypnotizing a person seemed like a rather harmless and amusing thing to do, despite the fact that nobody had the slightest idea what was actually occurring. A really showy hypnotist came equipped with a pocket watch to swing in front of the subject's face, and after a couple of minutes of laying the groundwork, he produced a person with a strong desire to peck like a chicken or sit on invisible chairs. The guests, who had now become the audience, considered this fabulous entertainment.

Bio amazing, indeed!

No doubt there are a few amateur hypnotists out there with no place to go on Saturday night because hypnotism is not the amusement it once was. It is serious stuff, but still as baffling and mysterious as ever. We can induce hypnotic trances left and right, but no one knows why it can be done or what exactly it is we are doing.

Hypnosis comes from a Greek word meaning "sleep," (that old god Hypnos again) which is rather unfortunate, because hypnosis is nothing at all like sleep. Under hypnosis you are awake and fully aware of your surroundings. You are conscious, but in a strange kind of trance state. We do know that a hypnotized person is usually very relaxed, highly sensitive to suggestion, and can tap into long forgotten memories. Most of us can be hypnotized if we want to be. All it takes is trust in the hypnotist and the ability to pay attention. If you decide to resist, you can.

Hypnotists don't swing pocket watches anymore to entrance you, mainly because they don't own them. Some do use gizmos, such as a coin or pencil, but they aren't really necessary. The idea is to get you to focus your attention on something so you will listen to the hypnotist's voice. Actually, you can just as effectively be put into a trance while your eyes are closed.

The hypnotist speaks softly, easing you into a trance by suggesting that you are relaxed, very relaxed, that your eyelids are growing heavy, that you can't keep them open anymore, that they are closing, closing, closing. . . . Somehow, this little technique does the trick, and in a short while you are in that bio amazing state we call the hypnotic trance.

Now, the first thing the hypnotist does is to find out how you respond to suggestion. So, if you'll kindly turn your attention to the fabulous Dr. Hypno and his nephew Gladstone, they will demonstrate this for you. (Notice how Gladstone's head has dropped to one side and that his eyes are closed.)

"Are you relaxed, Gladstone?"

"Yes."

"Good. Now, you are going to start feeling your right arm getting heavy. It is getting very heavy, Gladstone, heavier and heavier. Your right arm is getting so heavy that it will start feeling like lead, very heavy, just like lead. When I count to four, your arm will be just as heavy as lead. Ready? One, very heavy. Two, heavier and heavier. Three, almost as heavy as lead. And four. Your arm is so heavy, it is impossible for you to lift it."

With each suggestion, Gladstone has indeed felt his arm getting heavier, but now he is telling himself that he can lift his arm if he wants to. He is thinking, "I know I have been hypnotized, but so what? I'll just shoot my arm right into the air like a rocket, and then we'll see who's boss!"

But to his absolute surprise, Gladstone finds that he cannot lift his arm even the tiniest bit. Of course, there is nothing physically wrong with Gladstone's arm and Gladstone knows this, but Dr. Hypno's suggestion has registered somewhere in Gladstone's brain and created the "paralysis." In a sense, Gladstone was talked into it. Gladstone's brain allows this to happen because the suggestion was not unreasonable. (Silly, yes, but not unreasonable.) It did not offend or upset Gladstone or create a serious moral conflict within him.

Ah ha! But enter, stage left, the evil Dr. Demonico. In an oily voice, Dr. Demonico suggests that Gladstone approach Dr. Hypno and choke the life out of him. He presents his suggestion in stages, gradually planting and reinforcing the idea. Dr. Demonico is very good, and his voice is persuasive, but Gladstone stays put and refuses to carry out the dastardly suggestion. That's because he really doesn't want to. Even under hypnosis, Gladstone is still able to think, reason, and make decisions, and this is one suggestion he resists. In fact, Gladstone, who knows Dr. Demonico is off his nut, decides to end the hypnotic session and promptly brings himself out of his trance.

Hypnosis is not a permanent state, as Gladstone just illustrated. Gladstone became so dismayed and anxious over Dr. Demonico's hideous plan that he was able to "detrancify" himself. To put it another way, Gladstone stopped playing along. This would also have happened if there had been an emergency, such as a fire. Remember, a hypnotized person is conscious and aware of everything that is going on. The minute the flames broke out, Gladstone's survival instinct would have overridden the hypnosis (and the arm paralysis, too).

But suppose Dr. Demonico hypnotizes Gladstone and then, with a sneaky twirl of his moustache, leaves him that way. Out the door he goes, laughing that rotten, diabolical laugh of his. Is this the end of Gladstone as we know him? Is he trapped in a hypnotic trance forever? No, Gladstone is quite safe. In a little while, his trance will turn to drowsiness and finally to a deep sleep. Several hours later Gladstone will awaken normally.

As I mentioned, hypnosis has an astounding effect on memory. It seems to unlock the dustiest filing cabinets in our brain, giving us access to a wealth of information we didn't even know we had. It is believed that our brain absorbs everything we experience, no matter how small or unimportant. Some of these memories stand out clearly. Others are just under the surface, and with a little mental tugging, we can get at them. Most, though, are sent to Siberia because they are either too trivial, too painful, or have become too old. In some mysterious way, hypnosis allows us to pull our toughest memories from the dead file. Depending on the hypnotist's method, we either experience the event, or watch it unfold like a TV drama.

Recently, police departments have started using hypnosis to help them crack tough cases. Eyewitnesses almost always see far more than they consciously remember, and some of these details can be enormously important, especially when the police don't have many clues.

In 1976, hypnosis helped California police solve the famous Chowchilla kidnapping case. Bus driver Ed Ray and twenty-six school children had been kidnapped and held prisoner in a camouflaged ditch. Under hypnosis, Ray was able to recall the license number of the kidnapper's van.

In another case, a young lawyer who had had lye thrown in her face could not remember anything about her attacker. She had been badly scarred, and because of the trauma, had blocked out the memory. In addition, she had only gotten a brief glimpse of the man. Hypnotized, however, she was able to describe what he looked like, and based on the information she supplied, the man was arrested.

But hypnosis can play some tricks. When the only eyewitness to a 1981 murder in Joliet, Illinois, was unable to supply any details about the murderer's identity, he was hypnotized with the hope that his memory would be improved. The hypnotist instructed the man to zoom in on the murderer's face and describe what he saw. While entranced, the witness described a former classmate, who was then promptly arrested and put on trial for the murder. The testimony of the witness seemed quite good until an ophthalmologist took the stand. The doctor pointed out that since the murder had occurred at night, the furthest distance a person could see with any reliability was thirty feet. The witness, he said, had been nearly one hundred yards away, making it impossible for him to have seen facial details. The defense rested, and the suspect was released.

So what did hypnosis do if it did not enhance the man's memory? People under hypnosis are very suggestable. They are easy to convince, and they aim to please the hypnotist. Perhaps if the hypnotist suggests that the subject can remember something, the person will invent a memory. Even though the subject has no actual recall of an event, he or she will create details that pass for recall. For this reason, scientists urge police departments to tread very carefully when another person's life is at stake.

Perhaps the most fascinating phenomenon of the hypnotic trance is age regression. Age regression is a kind of time travel in the mind. The hypnotist suggests that you are going back in time, that the years are melting away, and that you are getting younger and younger.

"You are nine years old," you hear him say. "Do you see yourself as nine years old? Good, but you can go still farther back in time. Back and back and back. Now you are eight. You are eight years old."

Slowly, curiously, incredibly, your behavior and facial expressions are changing. You begin to fidget a little in your seat. You swing your legs as though they are too short to reach the floor.

"Can you tell me what you are wearing today?" asks the hypnotist.

You look down at your clothes and grin. "My pink party dress."

"It's very pretty," says the hypnotist as reinforcement. "Why are you so dressed up?"

"Today is my birthday. We're having a party."

"How old are you?"

"I'm six."

This is not play acting, here. You truly believe you have just turned six years old and that your birthday party is about to begin. You will see the guests arriving, even go through the motions of opening the presents you received that day. Since time for you will pass at its normal pace, the hypnotist might speed up the action by turning your attention to specific events—editing in a way.

Your brain, meanwhile, has done some editing of its own. It has sealed off your memory of everything that happened after your sixth birthday. This prevents "realtime" from seeping into "hypnotime" and upsetting the image you have of yourself as six years old. One part of your brain is tricking another part and doing it quite well indeed. If you hadn't yet learned to ride a bicycle at age six in realtime, you won't know how to do it at age six in hypnotime. This memory is released when the hypnotist brings you forward to the age at which you learned that skill.

One young man, suffering from epilepsy, was regressed to an age before the disease developed. His brain waves were being monitored and as soon as he reached his pre-epileptic age, his brain waves became normal. When he was brought forward, the epileptic wave patterns returned.

Another young man insisted he couldn't speak a word of Japanese, but when he was regressed to the age of four, he spoke Japanese fluently. At age six, he no longer knew the language. As it turned out, a grandparent had taught him Japanese when he was a child. He had spoken it constantly, but only for about two years, and today he doesn't remember a word of it.

You might be wondering if hypnotists can regress people all the way back to their actual birth. After all, being born was an experience, so it must be part of our memory bank. This dramatic regression has been tried, but the results were disappointing. As a newborn baby, the person was neither able to understand the hypnotist nor communicate.

But perhaps we can go a step further.

Many societies and religious groups believe in reincarnation. We have been here before, they say, in other places, other times, other bodies. (Reincarnate means "to make into flesh again.") You may once have been a Roman slave, or a Spanish conquistador, or a serving girl in England in the 1400's, or a soldier in Napoleon's army. You may have been a witch who was burned at the stake, a Neanderthal who was mauled by a sabre-toothed tiger, a passenger on the ill-fated *Titanic*.

An interesting idea, is it not?

Well, in November of 1952, amateur hypnotist Morey Bernstein regressed Virginia Tighe back, back, back through her childhood. At one year old, Bernstein suggested that she could go even further. Even further, he said, and she would begin to have memories of far-away lands. The minutes ticked by in realtime as Virginia drifted through hypnotic mindtime. At last, Bernstein addressed her.

"What is your name?"

Virginia stirred, and in a soft, Irish brogue she said, "Bridie. Bridie Murphy."

In six astonishing sessions, all recorded on tape, Bernstein learned that Bridie Murphy was born Bridget Kathleen Murphy on December 20, 1798. Her father had been a barrister (lawyer) named Duncan Murphy. Bridie had lived just outside Cork, in a place she referred to as "The Meadows," but had moved to Belfast after she had gotten married. She had had no children and had apparently died in 1864.

Well now, what have we here? Reincarnation or a lot of hooey?

It doesn't seem to be hooey for a number of reasons. First, Virginia had never been to Ireland nor had she ever read any books on the subject. True, Cork and Belfast are well-known, but "The Meadows" is something else. It sounded like a familiar name townspeople might call a local area. Did Virginia make this up? Apparently not. An old map of Cork drawn in 1801 showed a place called Mardike Meadows, and its location and geography fitted well with Virginia's description of The Meadows.

Then there were the two grocers—Farr and Carrigan—whom Bridie had supposedly dealt with. Indeed, a Belfast city directory for 1865–1866 listed Farr and Carrigan, grocers. Bridie also mentioned a tuppence, a small unit of currency. Amazingly, it was discovered that the tuppence was in circulation in Ireland at the time, *but only at that time.*

These details are important because they are so unimportant. How could Virginia Tighe know them? They are the kinds of facts she could almost certainly not have read in a book or learned from talking to people.

HOWEVER ...

Virginia's case is not airtight.

Item: Virginia had once lived across the street from a woman named Bridie Corkell who had been born in Ireland.

Item: Extensive research could find no evidence for the existence of Bridie Murphy or any member of her family.

Item: As Bridie, Virginia occasionally came out with modern American words such as "candy," and "downtown," unknown in nineteenth century Ireland.

THEN AGAIN ...

Historical proof of Bridie's family is almost impossible to obtain since no records were kept in that part of Ireland in the 1800s. As Bridie, Virginia constantly spoke with an Irish brogue and often used typical Irish expressions. When she wanted a handkerchief, for instance, she asked for a linen.

What all this means is anybody's guess. Did Virginia fashion her Bridie personality from bits and pieces of memories? The brain absorbs everything, remember, no matter how small and insignificant. Remember, too, under hypnosis people are highly suggestable. Did Bernstein, perhaps, suggest too much, and was Bridie Murphy Virginia's attempt to comply with Bernstein's wishes? Or did Virginia Tighe once exist as Bridie Murphy? After more than thirty years, this hypnotic journey into time is still unexplained.

And that, of course, is what makes it so bio amazing.

CHAPTER 5

The Hot Foot Caper

W hat you are about to read is no hoax. It's not a trick, an illusion, a fake, a phoney, an exaggeration, witchcraft, stagecraft, flimflam, or fraud. It has been practiced since ancient times and so far nobody has been able to figure out the secret. It is the bio amazing phenomenon of fire walking.

Regardless of what part of the world you see this done—Europe, Fiji, India, or Japan—the scenario is essentially the same. A large pit of perhaps forty feet by twenty feet is dug and lined with logs. Over this goes a layer of stones. The logs are set ablaze and allowed to burn for at least twenty-four hours. By then they have been reduced to ash, and the stones are glowing red hot.

The superheated air above the pit sways and shimmers like a cellophane curtain, forcing back the gathering spectators. Native attendants, drenched in sweat, move up and down the length of the trench, prodding the live coals with long sticks. The heat is so intense that the attendants must be doused often with buckets of cold water. Someone tosses a bit of colored cloth onto the hot stones, and it flares to nothingness, carbonized instantly by the fantastic temperature of the pit. It is hot enough to melt lead.

Suddenly, there is a faint rustling of leaves, and from the coolness of the forest come the fire walkers. They are barefoot. Solemnly, they approach the pit in single file. The crowd presses forward, expectant but fearful. One by one, the fire walkers step onto the flame-reddened rocks and begin to make their way across.

The spectators gasp in horrified disbelief. They grope mechanically for cameras hanging around their necks, tucked into overflowing totebags, dangling carelessly from wrists. Shutters snap in hysterical urgency. One woman hastily compares light readings with the man standing beside her. The folks back home won't believe this—men walking barefoot on hot coals! And look! It doesn't even seem to bother them!

The walkers are smooth and confident, never looking down, trusting their instincts and experience. There is no set path, no safe way across. Each man chooses his own route, feeling only for the rocks that will provide a solid footing. No one lingers, but no one rushes either. The walkers sweep like spirits over the furious hellfire, their eyes clear, their faces relaxed, their strides sure and graceful. In another place and time, they could almost be crossing a shallow stream, moving from rock to rock as the icy water swirls playfully around their ankles.

Already the spectators can see a fine layer of ash around the fire walkers' feet. A few people begin to whisper that the ash is probably acting as an insulator.

"How could it?" someone cries. "Those rocks must be at least 600°!"

At last the fire walkers reach the end of the pit. They step out, turn, and to the absolute amazement of the spectators, repeat their performance. In all, they will have gone eighty feet through something resembling the conditions of a blast furnace.

Now the frenzied crowd descends upon the fire walkers. They ebb and flow around them, reaching out to touch them, to convince themselves that they are human. The fire walkers are breathing heavily. Their hearts are thundering. Their clothes are soaked with sweat. The powdery ash is wiped from their ankles and feet, but there is nothing to be seen. No burns, no blisters, no marks of any kind. A woman grabs the sleeve of one of the pit attendants.

"How?" she asks. "How is this possible?"

The pit attendant shrugs. "Who can say? I have seen them walk the flames many times. Always it is the same. No one knows how. They just do it, that's all."

In one section of Greece, fire walking is part of an annual religious festival held in May on the Feast Day of a saint. The fire ceremony honors Saint Constantine who is said to be the fire walkers' protector. This belief dates back to 1250 when a raging fire swept through the Church of Saint Constantine in a small Greek village. According to the legend, some of the villagers heard the icons wailing and rushed into the church to save them. The nave and chancel were completely engulfed in flames, yet the villagers emerged unharmed. Since then, the descendants of these few villagers have held the fire walk every year to illustrate their faith in the continuing protection of Saint Constantine.

The walkers are a chosen few, carrying on the tradition of their ancestors. Hours of prayer is their sole preparation for the ceremony. They sit apart from the spectators—the deeply religious as well as the curious—while the pit coals burn to scarlet. The air pulses with haunting music from a drum and a lyre, two of the world's most ancient instruments.

And then, when all has been made ready, the fire walkers rise from their meditations and advance toward the flames. They carry images of Saint Constantine and Saint Helen, reproductions of the icons that have been passed down through scores of generations. The dance of fire begins and lasts until the burning coals have died to gray ash—about half an hour. Very few of the walkers suffer any injury, and those who do almost never have more than second-degree blistering.

The fire walkers of Greece maintain that their impossible feat is made possible through faith. Those who truly believe that it can be done are the ones who actually do it. The walkers, of course, feel something. They compare the sensation to walking on a prickly field, but deny that they feel the heat. In fact, they add, sometimes their feet even feel cool.

The fire walkers in the village of Sunderpur, India, also believe they are protected by a religious deity. She is the goddess Kali, who is represented as something of a she-monster with enormous powers.

The Fiji Islanders claim they are not even walking on the stones. The water god, they say, sends hundreds of water babies to lie down on the blazing fire and act as insulators. So the walkers never come in contact with the rocks because they are crossing the pit on the backs of the water babies.

Now, these rather poetic explanations may serve the fire walkers, but the more scientifically-minded find them inadequate, to say the least. Science never accepts the word magic as the answer to a problem, so attempts have been made to discover how the fire walkers are physically able to withstand temperatures that should literally be burning the flesh off their feet.

Probably the first, and certainly the most moronic, explanation of the fire walking phenomenon is that the rocks are not as hot as they appear. But time and again scientists have measured the pit temperature, and it is always in excess of 500° F. Sometimes it is as high as 800°. To understand how hot this is, think of the fact that lead will melt at about 600° F. Furthermore, if you have ever accidently splashed boiling water on yourself (212° F.), you know you can get a nasty burn. Pizzas are generally baked at about 500°, and you must surely have noticed what happens to the pepperoni, not to mention the cheese. So there is no point in quibbling over pit temperature. It's hot enough to do plenty of damage.

Next: sweat or ash act as insulators. While it is true that ash is present in some fire pits, it is by no means found in all of them. It depends on the kind of material being burned and the pit temperature. Sweat is part of the body's cooling system. It is primarily water and salt. Whether this simple mixture can provide enough insulation to protect the skin from 600° temperatures is doubtful.

The famous magician James Randi, who has watched a lot of fire walking ceremonies, believes it is the coals themselves that protect the fire walkers' feet. They are so hot, they create a dry steam blanket up to about the ankles, like invisible thermal shoes. If this is so, however, it should work all the time and for everyone who attempts the walk.

Curiously, success in the fire walk is a fickle thing. Tourists have tried it without preparation and without sharing the religious beliefs of their hosts. Some make it, some don't. Experienced fire walkers have a higher success rate, but they don't bat 1.000. In Fiji in the 1940s, one fire walker suffered such terrible burns that his legs had to be amputated.

A third suggestion has been that the walkers "do" something to their feet; for example, they smear on coconut oil or other mysterious balms. Actually, most fire walkers put absolutely nothing on their feet, and they have shown no objection to being examined before the walk. Hawaiian fire walkers traditionally wrap ti leaves (pronounced TEE) around their feet, however the plant hardly serves as protection. The leaves become ash almost the moment the walk begins.

Anthropologist Stephen Kane favors the theory of mind over matter. Fire walkers, he says, put themselves into a hypnotic trance. (Almost anyone can learn to do this.) Under hypnosis, the human body can be convinced of all kinds of things. But the fire walkers do more than short circuit the pain; they are actually able to prevent their flesh from burning. Amazingly, they can make their blood vessels constrict and even prevent their body from producing substances that cause blistering, burning, and swelling.

To support his theory, Kane points to the "cold feet" phenomenon. While watching a fire walking ceremony in Bora Bora, an American surgeon suddenly leaped up and bounded onto the fire pit. He could feel the intense heat all around him, he said, but his feet were cold! (Fifteen minutes after the walk, however, he was in agony.)

A scientist from the Max Planck Institute measured the "cold feet" phenomenon on a fire walker in the Fiji Islands. Temperature sensitive paint revealed that while the firepit was in excess of 600°, the firewalker's feet were, at the most, only 150°! So perhaps the special preparation made by nearly all the world's fire walkers is really a form of self-hypnosis. The mind controls the body.

But again, it must be pointed out that some people who decided, quite spontaneously, to make the fire walk suffered no ill effects. Did they "set" their mind to doing it without even realizing it?

The fire walking phenomenon in particular has shown us that the limits of what human beings are able to do are much broader than we originally thought. Athletes continue to break previous records which were once considered to be the outermost boundries. Endurance competitions have left us in awe of our own physical capabilities. The astonishing feats of Indian Yogis, accomplished almost exclusively through powerful mind control, leave us breathless.

It has been said that no human being ever lives up to his or her potential. According to science, we use a mere ten percent of our brain; the other ninety percent lies dormant—unnoticed, untouched, unexplored. So we cannot help but wonder, as we probe the mystery that is us, how high is up?

The Mystery
of the Idiot Savants

The next time you pass a fruit stand, think about this: the very thing that makes each of us absolutely unique weighs less than a bunch of bananas. It looks somewhat like a limp cauliflower and has the consistency of a handful of pomegranate seeds. It is, of course, the brain, commander in chief of all that is you.

Admittedly, the brain is not much to look at, but it wields more power than any other organ in the body. Without exception, everything you do—from blinking to composing a symphony—must go through Mr. Big first, so it isn't at all surprising that the brain enjoys maximum security. It sits in a tough casing that can be penetrated surgically by no less than a drill. The ancient Greeks, who thought the heart was the most important organ, should have guessed that anything so inaccessible as the brain had to be a real treasure.

The brain is the perfect machine. It has no moving parts, never needs oiling, and is highly compact and portable. Unfortunately, though, it doesn't come with blueprints, and that makes figuring out how it works an incredible challenge.

Recently, scientists have begun to make great strides in their understanding of which areas of the brain control specific movements. They have stimulated various points and been able to locate our speech and vision centers, our swallowing reflex, and so forth. They have even found what they believe to be our memory center—or at least one of its cubicles. But the toughest nuts of all to crack have been intelligence, creativity, and talent. What are they, exactly? How was, for example, Leonardo da Vinci's brain different from ours? What did Beethoven have that we don't have?

In an effort to discover those will-o'-the-wisps called thoughts and ideas, Albert Einstein, a rather smart cookie himself, requested that his brain be removed and studied after his death. Since Einstein is considered to have been a genius, it was hoped that his brain would somehow look different from everyone else's. Well, the lab tests went on for quite some time, but in the end they showed that there was really nothing extraordinary about Einstein's gray matter. In fact, if the sections hadn't been labeled Einstein, A., they might very easily have blended in with all the other samples.

So, the essence of intelligence still eludes us, but we have taken some fairly good shots at trying to measure it. Perhaps the most famous test for intelligence is the Stanford-Binet, which yields what is called an intelligence quotient, or I.Q. A person's I.Q. is represented by a number, and the higher the number, the greater the person's intellectual ability. About forty-five percent of us have an I.Q. between 90 and 110. This is considered average intelligence. A mere one percent of the population is above 140, and about three percent is below 70. While I.Q. tests are by no means perfect, they do serve as a gauge. They are designed to indicate potential, so if you imagine all of us as pole vaulters, you would expect the person with an I.Q. of 145 to be able to vault higher than someone with an I.Q. of 75. Makes sense, doesn't it? That is why science is thoroughly confused by the mystery of the idiot savants.

Savant is a French word that means "someone of great learning." An idiot is a person whose intellectual ability falls into the lowest I.Q. range. So when the words *idiot* and *savant* are used together, the phrase becomes a contradiction, and that is precisely the core of the problem. Without exception, all idiot savants are retarded, but in one or two very specific areas, they are geniuses.

Charles and George are identical twins. They have I.Q.'s somewhere between 60 and 70. George has been taught to read, write, and do arithmetic problems on the most basic level. Charles's skills are far fewer. But give the twins a date decades into the future and they can tell you how many days will pass until then. Sure, the math is simple. It only requires that you know how many days there are in each month and that you be able to add several two-digit numbers. A child in elementary school could do it. But how long would it take? A minute? Two minutes? Three minutes?

Charles and George can do this at about the same speed as a computer.

They can also tell you what day of the week that date will fall on and in what year that same day and date will coincide again.

Assume that this year January 14 was a Tuesday. Do you know when January 14 will again fall on a Tuesday? Does anybody know that? Provided the following year is not a leap year, the next January 14 will be a Wednesday. The year after that it will be a Thursday. January 14 will advance one day every year except on leap years when it will advance two days. Leap years occur every four years on even numbered years.

Are you still following all of this?

Well, it doesn't matter. Charles and George don't understand it either, but they always come up with the right answer. It takes them about half a second. Even more amazing, they are always right. Admittedly, this is not a very useful skill, but it is one that almost none of us has.

Charles and George are human calendars. Somehow, they know days and dates hundreds of years into the past and thousands of years into the future. A sample:

- Julius Caesar was killed on March 15, 79 A.D. What day of the week was that?

- What will be the first day of the year 2000?

- What is the date of the tenth Tuesday in the year 6501?

Apparently, George and Charles don't do any calculating at all. When asked how they do do it, their reply is simply, "It's in my head."

Do the answers just magically appear to them? Are they computing at light speed without even being aware of it? Nobody knows. But their uncanny ability is peanuts compared to what some idiot savants can do.

One young man could figure square roots. When you square a number, you multiply the number by itself. When you figure a square root, you start with the square. What multiplied by itself equals, say, 16? Finding square roots requires some tricky division, and, with pencil and paper, takes a fair amount of time to do. So now try to imagine somebody figuring square roots of four-digit numbers in four seconds. Even a college math professor probably can't do it without a calculator. Do you realize how short four seconds is? And this same idiot savant could do cube roots in six seconds. A cube root asks the magic question, "What number multiplied by itself *twice* will give you such and such a number?"

Clearly, this is extremely sophisticated stuff for someone who could barely do basic arithmetic. But it didn't stop there. When the boy was given a number, he could double it and keep on doubling it at almost superhuman speed. Two plus two is four, plus four is eight, plus eight is sixteen, plus sixteen is thirty-two, plus thirty-two is sixty-four. . . .

Well, enough of that. You've got the idea.

In the eighteenth century, idiot savant Jedediah Buxton, who knew no arithmetic at all, pulled off this little stunner. Some friends had taken him to the theatre and after the performance, Buxton's sole comment was a kind of weird census report. He casually informed everyone of the exact number of words spoken by the actors and the total number of steps taken by the dancers.

Even more remarkable are the idiot savants who show an astonishing talent in the arts. Yoshihiko Yamamoto is one of Japan's leading artists. He went from simply copying cartoons to creating polished, finely drawn sketches literally overnight. Yamamoto has an I.Q. of 40.

J. H. Pullen's talent lay in draftsmanship and engineering. Pullen designed and built a ten-foot model of a ship he called *The Great Eastern*. Every single detail of the ship was specified in the reams of preliminary drawings he did. When he saw it would take two million two hundred and twenty-five thousand wooden pins to fix the planks to the frame of the ship, he built a machine to make the pins! At the time Pullen was doing all of this, he was a resident of the Earlwood Asylum, a home for the retarded.

One twenty-two-year-old man could repeat passages read to him in Danish, Japanese, and Greek. His accent and rhythm were perfect, although he couldn't speak a word or understand any of the languages.

Then there's Harriet who lives in Boston. One day, out of the clear, blue sky, she started playing classical piano pieces. She can listen to a composition for the first time and tell you when it was written. She can take "Happy Birthday" and play it in the style of Chopin, or Bach, or Strauss. She knows chords, keys, octaves—the works! How? She never had a music lesson in her life, and her I.Q. is way below normal.

Still, the most amazing story of all concerns an idiot savant named Leslie who was born retarded, without eyes, and a victim of cerebral palsy. Leslie was abandoned by his biological parents and adopted from a Milwaukee hospital by May and Joe Lemke at the age of six months. Leslie was as unresponsive to the world around him as a rubber doll, and the doctors told the Lemkes he didn't have long to live. Nevertheless, May and Joe worked overtime to enrich Leslie in a variety of ways—talking and singing to him, cuddling him, later teaching him to move his limbs, and finally to walk. He was sixteen years old when he took his first steps.

But it was a piece of string that changed the course of events for Leslie. The string was wrapped around a package and when May saw Leslie plucking at it, she got the idea of introducing him to music. From that moment on, sonatas, arias, overtures, concertos poured from the radio, the record player, the television. May bought a secondhand piano and put it in Leslie's bedroom. She placed Leslie's fingers on the keys and showed him how to produce sounds. She saturated him with music of every conceivable kind, but as always, Leslie remained mute and indifferent.

Then it was winter, 3:00 A.M., and Tchiakovsky's Piano Concerto No. 1 was filling the house. It flowed through the darkened rooms like a rising wave, rich, powerful, magnificent. May and her husband bolted from their bed, and there at the piano sat Leslie, his fingers expertly flying over the keys, playing notes he had heard perhaps only two or three times before on the radio.

What extraordinary event had taken place inside Leslie's brain? He cannot read, write, or carry on a thoughtful conversation, yet he performs classical music, jazz, gospel, rock, country and western, and ragtime. He can sing Italian operas without missing a single note or word. He gives concerts to standing-room-only audiences and receives thunderous applause—not because he's handicapped, but because he's incredibly talented.

And yet, all the intelligence tests say Leslie should not be able to do any of this.

None of the idiot savants are supposed to have even a shred of talent or creativity. Their mental development is that of a five year old or less.

Science admits it is completely baffled by the idiot savant phenomenon, but it has, as you would expect, taken its best shot at the problem. One important clue, say the scientists, may be the idiot savant's ability to concentrate. Twenty-four hours a day we are being bombarded by information streaming into our brain. All of this input is very distracting. We have to do a juggling routine—pay attention to this, ignore that, notice the other thing but file it away for later, and so on. It's like a water faucet that's turned on full.

But for the idiot savant, the world is a faucet that is only dripping a little. Idiot savants don't process as much information as the rest of us because they can't, so they have far fewer distractions. With fewer distractions, they are able to concentrate deeply on one thing. What that one thing is may depend on which area of their brain is working to capacity. Maybe mental retardation is not a general dulling, but more like scattered power blackouts.

It is also interesting to note that creativity and original thinking do not necessarily depend on intelligence (whatever that is!). In a sample group, students with high I.Q.'s scored *lower* on a creativity test than students whose I.Q.'s were in the average range. In other words, you don't have to be an "egghead" to have talent. The best example of this is Albert Einstein, whose teachers hardly noticed him in the classroom.

One even shook his head and sadly said, "Tsk, tsk. I fear, Albert, you will never amount to anything."

Indeed!

So we are right back where we started, puzzling over that funny-looking organ with all the loops and folds. Somewhere among those snaky recesses lie the sources of our intelligence, our talents, and our ideas. And somewhere lies the solution to the mystery of the idiot savants.

CHAPTER 7

Acupuncture: A Case in Point

A twenty-six-year-old woman is brought into a Nanking, China, hospital after a serious infection has left her crippled and bedridden. For the past year she has been treated with what the Chinese call "western drugs," but they haven't been effective. The woman remains in great pain and unable to walk.

In the hospital, the woman begins a program of acupuncture treatments. Needles are inserted in her back, thigh, and legs once a day for ten days. For three days she receives no acupuncture and then resumes the treatment for another ten days. In one month, the woman is out of bed and walking with the support of two nurses. By the end of the third ten-day treatment, she is walking alone. At four months, the pain is gone and there are no signs of illness.

Two men sit in a dentist's office, each waiting to have a tooth pulled. The dentist enters, approaches the first man, and inserts an acupuncture needle in his cheek. He rotates the needle for less than half a minute, says the Chinese equivalent of "Open wide," and pulls the tooth. The man nods and smiles. He has felt nothing.

No needle is necessary with the second patient. The dentist uses the tip of his forefinger to apply pressure to an area on the man's cheek. A short time later the dentist is ready. "Open, please." Out comes the tooth, swiftly and painlessly.

Chou Zhong-ping, a forty-four-year-old office worker, is wheeled into surgery to have a tumor removed from his lung. The only injection he receives is a muscle relaxant. At 9:20 an acupuncturist inserts a long needle into Zhong-ping's right forearm and begins twirling it vigorously.

9:40. The surgeons make the first incision. It is very deep, but Zhong-ping feels nothing. The surgeons spread the ribs and begin to probe for the tumor. Zhong-ping lies quietly but alert, listening to the sounds of his chest operation. He smiles and assures everyone that he is in no pain.

11:00. The surgeons close the chest.

11:05. The acupuncturist withdraws the needle, leaving only a small, bloodless mark.

Zhong-ping is gently transferred to a gurney, and as he is wheeled out of the operating room, he waves to the surgeons.

This is what acupuncture can do. It is a treatment, a cure, an anesthetic for pain. It has been practiced in China for over three thousand years, obviously because it works, but no one knows why.

Acupuncture itself is amazingly simple. Ultra-thin needles are inserted into the skin to a depth of about half an inch. When used as a treatment for disease or as a substitute for Novocain, the needles are left in place for a few minutes. As a surgical anesthetic, the needles must be rotated for the duration of the operation. Nowadays, this rotation is done electronically. Finally, the needles are withdrawn, quite painlessly and with almost no blood, and except for the part where the patient thanks the acupuncturist, that's the entire procedure.

The theory behind acupuncture, though, is a little more complicated. To the untrained eye, needle placement may look like grab and jab, but it most certainly is not. Chinese texts have identified several hundred specific acupuncture points. The points are located along tracks called meridians, rather like train stations on the MTA. With just two exceptions, the meridians occur in pairs, twelve on the right side of the body matching twelve on the left side. The two unpaired meridians are in the center and said to be the most important because they contain the greatest amount of yin and yang.

The concept of yin and yang is the foundation of Chinese philosophy. Yin and yang represent all the opposites in the universe—light and dark, hot and cold, male and female, etc. Each of us has a certain amount of yin and yang, and as long as the amounts are equal, we are healthy. Sometimes, though, this balance is upset, and when we have too much yin or too much yang, the result is illness.

Now, each meridian is related to a major organ, such as the heart, or lungs, or spleen, and each organ is either yin or yang. So what acupuncture tries to do is stimulate the organ that is responsible for knocking the yin and yang out of whack. When the balance is restored, the patient gets better.*

If all this sounds like a science fiction story, consider the following: Scientists have found that the meridians in acupuncture run parallel to the major nerves in the body. This interesting little fact has gotten some people to thinking that maybe the acupunc-

---

* Atoms, the basic building blocks of matter, are also in balance. They are composed of three kinds of particles: protons, with a positive charge; electrons, with a negative charge; and neutrons, which are neutral. In every atom the number of protons must equal the number of electrons so there is an electrical balance. Quite a coincidence, wouldn't you say? Makes you stop and think, especially since acupuncture is three thousand years older than the atomic theory.

ture points are trigger areas. Hit the trigger area and the body produces its own brand of medicine—a human vending machine! We do, in fact, manufacture natural pain killing substances called endorphins, and acupuncture just might have found the turn-on switch.

Certainly one of the worst kinds of headaches is the migraine. Dr. Felix Mann, a London physician, tells of one patient who had been plagued with migraines twice a week for twenty years. Dr. Mann administered ten acupuncture treatments using only two points—in the head and behind the knee—and achieved pretty impressive results. The patient went from an average of about 700 migraines a year to only four! And don't forget about Chou Zhong-ping and his lung operation or the two men who had their teeth pulled with acupuncture as the sole anesthetic.

Acupuncture has also been used during brain operations. In 1979, American doctors witnessed delicate surgery to remove a tumor of the pituitary gland. This walnut-sized gland, one function of which is to regulate growth, is located at the base of the brain. A single acupuncture needle was inserted in the patient's cheek as an anesthetic. The surgeons shaved the man's head, drilled through the skull, dug deep into the brain with scalpels, and extracted the tumor. Although the brain itself has no feeling, the scalp most certainly has. Yet, the patient, wide awake through the whole procedure, apparently felt nothing. Dr. Nathan Kaplan of the

University of California San Diego Medical School said, "I wouldn't have believed it if I hadn't looked at it myself."

In addition to being an effective anesthetic, acupuncture is also a treatment and a cure. Good results have been reported with cases of malaria, high blood pressure, asthma, heart disease, paralysis, arthritis, deafness, and infections. But are all these just impressive examples of mind over matter? Most of the great success stories come to us from China, where acupuncture has been practiced for thousands of years and where it is deeply imbedded in the culture and philosophy. Couldn't it be argued, then, that acupuncture only works on people who believe in it? Is the effect purely psychological, like a sugar pill?

Well, let us move to the Veteran's General Hospital in Taiwan where Dr. Chieh Chung receives a patient with a most unusual complaint. The man is an amputee suffering from phantom limb pain. Phantom limb pain is one of the great mysteries of medicine. The amputee experiences terrible pain in the missing limb—not the stump, mind you, but the arm, or hand, or foot that is *no longer there*. It occurs most often in people who have suffered long-term pain before the limb was amputated, but it is not unknown in sudden trauma victims; soldiers, for example, whose amputation occurred on the battlefield.

Dr. Chung's patient has come to the hospital only as a last resort. He doesn't think too much of acupuncture, but his pain is excruciating, and since all other treatments have failed, he has decided he has nothing to lose by trying it.

Dr. Chung carefully inserts the stainless steel needles at the five prescribed points, and the man's pain vanishes almost immediately. Relief is only temporary, though, and when the pain returns, so does Dr. Chung's patient. (This is not unusual. Several treatments are often required.)

Now, this time, Dr. Chung uses *ten* needles and deliberately inserts them at the *wrong* points. The fake acupuncture has no effect. The man, perhaps a bit confused by now, reports that he still has pain. So out come the ten needles, in go five new ones at the correct points, and the man's face tells the whole story. His pain is gone.

A similar experiment was conducted at the University of Washington by Dr. C. Richard Chapman. The volunteers were medical students who were given painful shocks directly into the nerve of their teeth. If you do not take Novocain during a drilling expedition at the dentist's office, you may have experienced a sudden eyeball-loosening blast of pain when the drill accidently hits a nerve. This is what Chapman's medical students subjected themselves to.

When Chapman stimulated the phony acupuncture points and then administered the electric shock, the brave volunteers hit the proverbial ceiling. However, when the correct acupuncture points were stimulated, the students reported no pain.

Further proof that acupuncture has nothing to do with the patient's belief in the procedure comes from veterinarians. Animals, it seems, respond to acupuncture treatments just as well as humans.

Acupuncture is far from magical. It does indeed cause changes in the body. In addition to stimulating the release of our natural pain-killing chemicals, it raises skin temperature, alters blood pressure, dilates (widens) the blood vessels, and affects digestion. So acupuncture is apparently pressing the right buttons, and someday we may discover why.

CHAPTER 8

The Mystery
of the Miracle Cures

There is a beautiful church in Canada called the Church of Saint Anne de Beaupré. On any given day it is certain to be crammed with a curious combination of worshippers, tourists, and, most significantly, ill and crippled people. The church is a holy shrine, and miracles of healing are said to occur there. Braces and crutches hang from the large pillars just inside the entrance, discarded by those who came and were supposedly cured. The scene is so extraordinary, even dyed-in-the-wool skeptics are apt to be strangely moved.

Lourdes in France is the world's most famous shrine. It receives countless numbers of people every year who journey many miles hoping for a miracle.

Lourdes is the spot where an illiterate peasant girl, Marie Bernarde Soubirous, reportedly saw several visions of the Virgin Mary in 1858. Although Marie, who was very sickly most of her life, never claimed a cure, others did, and Lourdes became a place of pilgrimage.

The cures at Lourdes, Saint Anne de Beaupré, Our Lady of Fátima in Portugal, and other such shrines are said to be the result of faith. It is a miracle from God that the blind are given sight, the deaf their hearing, and the crippled the power to walk. These healings, which are quite often sudden, do indeed happen, and they have been documented, both by eyewitnesses and responsible medical professionals.

A faith cure occurs if a person recovers when there is no physical possibility for a recovery. For example, if blindness is caused by the destruction of the optic nerve, the blindness is permanent. The optic nerve carries visual impulses to the brain. When it is not functioning, the brain cannot "see" the picture the eye receives. It's like taking a photograph and then throwing away the film. Without an optic nerve, there is absolutely no physical way the person can be made to see.

Faith healing is accomplished without drugs, surgery, physical therapy, or medical procedures of any kind. When there is a human healer, the person may pray, touch the patient (laying on of hands), or go into a trance, but not so much as a bandage is ever used. The cure is effected through faith, the will of God, or what is sometimes called "cosmic energy."

Perhaps one of the most charismatic faith healers who ever lived was Kathryn Kuhlman. Kuhlman's services were always mobbed. People came on crutches, in wheelchairs, weakened by multiple sclerosis, dying from cancer, paralyzed, arthritic, blind, deaf, feverish, wracked with pain, deformed, hobbling, shuffling, and carried in the arms of others, desperately hoping to be cured of their afflictions.

Most of them were not.

It all looked promising and hopeful during the service as Kuhlman stood before the throng in a long white dress, her graceful arms raised skyward, shouting, "Someone in the back with diabetes! The power of God is flowing through you! You are being cured!" Or, "Someone in the balcony is wearing a hearing aid. Remove it! You can hear!"

And then, "Stand up! Those of you who are cured, stand up! Come forward!"

Invariably, there would be a flood of people.

"Is this your wheelchair?" to a man crippled with arthritis.

"Yes."

"Bend over! Touch your toes! Raise your arms!"

And incredibly, the man would do it, his beaming face filled with the emotion of the moment. The audience would cheer his miracle, praying that they would be the next to throw down their canes and approach the stage. But Kuhlman's assistants never followed up on the man with arthritis, and so, nobody knew that the day after the service, the man was in his wheelchair as always.*

Dr. William Nolen, a physician from Minnesota, attended one of Kuhlman's services in the 1970s and tracked down several people who had claimed cures. Here are just a few.

A woman with multiple sclerosis: No one knows the cause of this disease or how to cure it. The symptoms and severity vary greatly from patient to patient. In addition, the symptoms appear in cycles. Sometimes they are much worse than at other times. There is no evidence that this woman's MS was arrested, and it was certainly not cured because the symptoms still exist today.

A man with cancer: He died six months after the service.

A man with migraine headaches: A migraine is a tightening and then a relaxation (paralysis) of the blood vessels in the head. It seems to be related to tension, but there may be other causes. People with migraines treat them in various ways—sleep, cold compresses on the eyes, aspirin, even Coca-Cola. Sometimes the treatments work, sometimes they don't.

This man reported fewer and less severe migraines after Kuhlman's service. Admittedly, this was an im-

---

* Kuhlman saw no reason to check on the progress of any of the people who claimed cures. It was not she who did the healing, she said, but God, and her faith in Him was absolute.

provement, but migraines are so unpredictable, we really can't attribute the improvement to Kuhlman.

Although Kuhlman's effectiveness is questionable, a handful of people who came in contact with her apparently did recover from severe illnesses.

In 1959, Myrtle Joseph was diagnosed as having chronic lymphatic leukemia. By 1964, she was getting regular blood transfusions. In 1967, Mrs. Joseph wrote to Kuhlman asking for her prayers. A short time later, Mrs. Joseph underwent a series of tests. All traces of the leukemia were gone. Her blood count was normal. In 1970, she celebrated her eightieth birthday.

In July, 1970, Venus Yates was in the intensive care unit of the Los Angeles County General Hospital. She was suffering from rheumatoid arthritis (no known cause or cure), rheumatic fever, and a spinal tumor. (Please note: not all tumors are malignant.) Venus was taken on a stretcher to one of Kuhlman's monthly healing sessions in the Shrine Auditorium in Los Angeles. At the end of the service, Venus's mother announced, quite spontaneously, that her daughter had been cured. Medical tests done a short time later on Venus were all negative.

Why did Venus Yates and Myrtle Joseph get better? Was the power of God working through Kuhlman?

Every now and then, doctors witness a recovery that they would have given million-to-one odds against. They are quick to add, however, that they don't know everything about the human body. Dr. William Nolen says that doctors are not healers. They only set the stage so that the body can heal itself. Drugs stimulate the body's own defenses, like a sergeant ordering the troops into action. Healing, then, is done from the inside out. We're in control.

It has been shown that many illnesses are either caused or greatly affected by our emotions. Scientists call this the mind-body connection. Everybody knows that people who lead very stressful lives are better candidates for high blood pressure, ulcers, heart disease, and stroke than people who take it easy. A number of things happen to our body when we experience stress. First, our chemistry changes. We produce more adrenaline, for example. Like a car engine that runs most efficiently with just the right air/gas mixture, we must have balanced chemical levels. If we allow ourselves to be affected by stress, we cause an imbalance. Second, physical changes occur. Muscles contract, blood pressure rises, heartbeat increases, pupils dilate, our stomach produces more digestive juices, and we begin to sweat.

All of this is the result of the "fight or flight" syndrome. Thousands of years ago, our cave-dwelling ancestors were faced with really only one kind of stressful situation: the attack of a large, wild animal, such as a saber-toothed tiger. Now, the cave dweller could either fight the animal or flee from it. Fighting and fleeing would each require extra strength and endurance, more than is usually needed for everyday activities. So the body responded with increased adrenaline levels, more powerful heart action, and so on.

We don't have to deal with saber-toothed tigers anymore, but we still have stress, and our body responds in the old-fashioned way. Unfortunately, though, we are not equipped to handle these bodily changes for any extended period of time. In other words, revving at 2000 RPMs for too long will ruin our engine, and since constant stress revs our engine, it is harmful. After a while, things begin to break down.

Fear is perhaps the greatest stress we can experience. You've heard the phrase, "to die of fright," but it is more than just a phrase. People can actually die of severe stress brought on by terror.

The Australian Aborigines practice a weird but effective kind of death by psychology called bone pointing. The weapon is a kundela, a finely honed human bone which is supposedly charged with psychic energy during an elaborate ceremony. Whenever a man breaks a tribal taboo, such as incest, he must receive the sentence of the kundela.

Usually, the man flees the village and must then be hunted by the kurdaitcha, or hit men. The condemned man knows the kurdaitcha will find him no matter what it takes, and for this reason alone he is as good as dead. As he scurries through the tall grasses, darting this way and that, trying to elude discovery, his terror is mounting. He can almost hear the soft crunch of footsteps behind him. His muscles are tense, his ears

straining for the smallest sound, his sleepless eyes prob-
ing the darkness. The deadly magic of the kundela has
already begun to work.

When the kurdaitcha finally tree their quarry—
sometimes after a pursuit that lasts for years—one of
the hit men drops to his knees and points the kundela
at the condemned man. Terror courses through the
victim's body, and he freezes like ice. Not one finger is
ever laid on him, and yet a few weeks later, the man is
dead, a victim of terror, stress, and his own emotions.

If our emotions can harm us in such a dramatic way,
they should also be able to alter our body chemistry
enough to cure many of our illnesses.

Some years ago at the Travis Air Force Base in California, Dr. Carl Simonton taught one hundred fifty-two
cancer patients to focus on the destruction of their cancer three times a day. The patients were asked to con-
jure up a specific image of the cancerous mass—as a slab
of raw liver, for example. Then they were told to
imagine that a teeming army of white blood cells was
descending on the enemy and carrying it away bit by
bit. The patients also received radiation therapy.

Simonton's results: The twenty patients who used
the mental attack strategy had an excellent response to
the radiation. All but two patients who either did not
use the strategy or used it only half-heartedly showed
poor response to the treatments. Dr. Simonton says he
"strongly believes that health is influenced by the
patient's mental attitude."

Indeed, more and more studies are showing that

people who express their emotions, who "get it off their chest," and "let it all out," have fewer physical complaints than people who keep their feelings inside. Crying, shouting, and laughing, it seems, are healthy. Screaming is good for the lungs. When you scream, you are forcing out more carbon dioxide than you would exhale normally. Laughing raises your blood pressure, increases your heartbeat, and stimulates your adrenaline and endorphin production. When you stop laughing, these levels fall very quickly, and the sudden plunge relieves stress. As for crying, that's beneficial, too. Tears, as you probably know, are a natural eyewash, but they also rid the body of toxins.

It is believed that emotions are responsible for nearly every cure claimed at holy shrines and under the encouraging eyes of faith healers. Many ailments respond surprisingly well to dramatic changes in our psychological state. The list includes cancer, migraine headaches, multiple sclerosis, acne and related skin ailments, intestinal disorders, heart disease, eye problems, hearing impairments, arthritis, bursitis, backaches and sciatica, and a host of others. As we readjust our thinking, we readjust our chemistry. The human body has a built-in pharmacy with acids, bases, salts, hormones, proteins, enzymes, all neatly tucked away in tiny bio flasks. When we laugh, we pull the stoppers of at least two of these flasks. Will we someday learn to uncork all the others? Are we on the very brink of learning part of the secret right now?

Consider the phenomenon of what is being called

psychic healing. Psychic healing involves meditation, either on the part of one person or a group of people whose combined energies are focused on the patient. Unlike faith healing, there is no mention of God whatsoever, and the meditation is closer to positive thinking than it is to praying.

Some years ago, a man was critically ill with a intestinal disease. His doctors admitted they could do nothing for him and that nature would have to take its own course. A short time later, a psychic healer visited the young man at the request of one of his relatives. The healer spoke briefly with the man and then spent about fifteen minutes in silent meditation at his bedside. Every day thereafter, she and her husband devoted twenty minutes to meditation on the young man and his condition. Six weeks later, the doctors announced that the young man's intestines had begun to heal. Today there is no trace of illness.

In 1974, a group meditation was practiced on a boy named Michael whose spinal nerves had been severed in a trampoline accident. Michael was left paralyzed from the neck down. The group was shown Michael's picture and given a brief description of the boy's personality, interests, and lifestyle prior to the accident. Then the group fell to silent meditation. According to reports, an hour later, Michael felt sensation in his toes for the first time. Although bound to a wheelchair, Michael has since regained some muscle function from the waist up.

Skeptics will argue that Michael's nerves had most

likely begun to repair themselves, and maybe they did, but the possible effects of meditation should not be dismissed lightly. Meditation has been shown, time and again, to bring about dramatic changes in the body. It lowers blood pressure, slows breathing and heartbeat, affects nerve function, relaxes muscles, and touches nearly every biological system in one way or another. Psychologist Lawrence Le Shan, who has been examining the psychic healing phenomenon, believes that the mind plays a vital role in the healing process. If we can project this "mental energy," that is, send it telepathically, we can then speed up the healing process in others.

Psychic healing appears remarkable, almost unbelievable, but there is no physical reason why it should not be possible. Believe it or not, it doesn't violate any of the known laws of physics. Spontaneous cures may be unexplained, but only because we know so little about this extraordinary phenomenon called life. It is a great jigsaw puzzle, many of whose pieces are still missing, but all of whose pieces are discoverable. And someday we may very well find that we not only produce our own medicine, but that we create our own miracles.

CHAPTER 9

The Case That Turned to Ashes

Victim #1:
Ipswich, England, April 9, 1744

Mrs. Grace Pett would not have liked the idea that her daughter discovered her body. Mrs. Pett also would not have liked the way she looked. She was burned beyond recognition. Her flesh had bubbled and sizzled and finally turned to ash. Her graying—well, slightly graying—hair had burst into flames, framing her head in a hideous yellow halo until there was nothing left to burn anymore. She was a deformed black mass, dumped on the floor of her neat and tidy sitting room.

They investigated, of course, and the verdict was death by fire of unknown cause. The furniture had not been touched, nor the curtains, nor the book that the late Mrs. Pett had been reading, nor the floor on which she had probably fallen.

"Curious," they said. "Most curious," and closed the case.

And Mrs. Pett would not have liked that idea at all.

Victim #2:
England, 1938

WOMAN DIES IN MYSTERY FIRE

Reuters. July 30, 1938 Mary Carpenter died yesterday in a mysterious fire while cruising the Norfolk Broads with family and friends. According to witnesses, Mrs. Carpenter suddenly burst into flames and was consumed within minutes. Family members insist they were unable to aid Mrs. Carpenter due to the speed and intensity of the fire. The railing and nearby deck chairs were untouched. The cause of the fire is still unexplained.

Victim #3:
St. Petersburg, Florida, 1951

With all his years on the force, the detective thought he had seen everything. He hadn't.

"All right," he barked at one of the officers. "What have we got?"

Mechanically, the officer read from a little pad. " 'Reeser, Mary Hardy. Age approximately sixty-five.' " He pointed to a grisly sight on the floor. "That's her."

The detective swallowed hard. He really thought he had seen everything. "Go on."

"The armchair was completely burned. Oh . . . except for the springs. Pretty weird. That stuff on the ceiling is like an oily soot. They took a sample. Same for the walls, only it doesn't go any higher than about four feet."

The detective chomped down hard on his unlit cigar. "Witnesses?"

"Not exactly," replied the officer, "but a few people you ought to talk to. You want to start with the landlady? Name's Carpenter."

The detective crossed the room and nodded to the coroner who had just arrived. "The minute you're done, doc."

"You'll be the first."

The detective stepped over the threshold into the hot Florida sun. The landlady was waiting outside with a uniformed officer.

"Mrs. Carpenter?"

The woman nodded. She was upset but under control, and the detective thanked God for small favors. "Want to tell me what happened?"

The landlady swallowed. "I didn't see it happen," she said, "but around five this morning I smelled smoke. I guess it must have awakened me. It wasn't really that strong. Just a faint sort of odor." She shrugged. "Well, I didn't think too much of it because there's this water pump in the garage that's been overheating lately, so I figured it was doing it again. I got up, went to the garage, turned off the pump, and went back to bed."

"The smell of smoke didn't get any stronger?" asked the detective.

"No. In fact, when I got up again an hour later . . ."

"That would be about six o'clock?"

"Yeah. Six or a little after. When I got up the smell was gone."

"Go ahead."

"Then at about eight o'clock this telegram came for Mary. Mrs. Reeser, I mean. Well, I signed the receipt and went to her apartment to give her the telegram. I started to turn the doorknob, and I had to pull my hand away because the thing was so hot. I got scared and thought the place was on fire, so I started screaming for help."

The detective shifted his cigar. "You didn't see flames?"

The landlady shook her head. "No. Nothing." She turned and pointed to a house across the street. "There were some painters over there, and when they heard me screaming they came running over. One of them got the door open and went inside."

"You didn't go in?"

"No. I guess I was afraid of what I would find."

"All right," said the detective. He motioned to the

uniformed officer who had moved back several paces. "We'll probably want to talk to you again Mrs., ah..."

"Carpenter."

"Yes. I'm sorry. Mrs. Carpenter." He nodded vaguely, awkwardly, to the landlady and moved off.

Already the detective was beginning to feel he would get nowhere with this case. He wondered how the coroner was doing and was tempted to hold off questioning the painters, but he hated the idea of going back into the house. God! The remains were hideous! He shook the image from his mind. He really thought he'd seen everything.

As expected, the painters weren't very much help. When they had opened the door, they had been hit with a blast of hot air. One of them had gone in and looked around but hadn't found anybody. He said the house had been a little smoky, but the only fire he saw was on a wooden ceiling beam between the living room and the kitchen. He had called the fire department and left after the trucks arrived. The firemen had discovered Mrs. Reeser after their search of the premises.

The detective steeled himself and went back into the apartment. He could hardly wait to hear what the coroner had to say.

"So, doc?" he said, clapping him on the shoulder.

The coroner wheeled. "You won't like it."

"Let me have it anyway," said the detective.

The coroner shook his head. "I swear, I thought I'd seen everything, but this! Whew! There's not much left. We've got a charred liver still attached to a small section of the vertebra. We've got a foot with a bedroom slipper still on it. And we've got a head, severely burned, shrunk down to the size of an orange. Wanna see it?"

The detective made a face. "A shrunken head?" he squawked.

"Yeah. Impossible, but there it is. Obviously it was death by fire, but what a fire! Say, 3000° at least. You got any ideas?"

"Are you kidding? I hate all of them: murder, accidental death, arson, suicide. Nothing washes. And how do you get a fire going 3000° and keep the whole place from going up?"

The coroner shrugged. "Good question."

The detective ran his fingers through his hair. "Just send me your report."

"Sure thing. Hey, you guys! Watch what you're doing with that head!"

The detective rolled his eyes. Eugh! he thought. Why would anybody ever want to be a coroner?

The air conditioner was going full blast, but the detective, hunched over his typewriter, was sweating. *Mrs. Reeser's death*, he typed, *was caused* . . . He stopped. Was caused by what? The coroner's report didn't help at all. When he put all the facts together they didn't make any sense. He stared helplessly at the official police form. He had to write something! He flipped through the coroner's report for the twentieth time. " 'Accidental death by fire of unknown origin,' " he read. "That's good. That's really good."

He picked up the FBI report and shook it angrily. "And this is a beauty, too! Mrs. Reeser's weight is estimated at 175 pounds but the remains, counting the skull and liver, don't even make ten pounds! For crying out loud! Is this some kind of science fiction story?"

"Talking to yourself again, Sarge?"

The detective looked up. "I need a vacation," he moaned.

The officer dropped a piece of paper onto the cluttered desk. "More on the Reeser case. It's from William Krogman, the forensic expert. You interested?"

The detective snatched up the paper.

Based on the condition of the victim, the fire was probably twice as hot as the average house fire. With this extreme temperature, the apartment should have been an inferno. The intense heat should also have caused the victim's head to burst, not shrink.

"Oh Brother!" cried the detective. "It gets worse!"

He turned back to the typewriter and reread what he had written. *Mrs. Reeser's death was caused . . .* He fished for the w . . . . *when a cigarette ignited her highly flammable nightgown.*

Angrily, he pulled the page out of the machine,

signed it, and pitched his mangled cigar into the waste-basket.

"Rats!" he growled. "I'm goin' to lunch!"

Victim #4:
Maybelle Andrews, London, England, late 1950s

"You understand this is only a coroner's inquest. It's not a trial."

"Yes," replied the young man.

"Tell us what you saw."

The young man swallowed. "Well, we were in the nightclub. We were dancing. Then all of a sudden she just caught fire. I can't believe it! She just caught fire! These bluish flames shot out from her neck and chest. I didn't even touch her. I swear!" The young man hid his face in his hands. "It was awful," he mumbled. "The fire just swallowed her up. I couldn't do anything. It happened in a second."

"Was anyone smoking? Was there a fire source nearby?"

"No," said the young man. "Nothing. Nothing at all. No one was smoking, and there weren't any candles on the table or anything. I didn't see her dress catch fire. The flames just seemed to burst outward, you know? From inside her body. I know that sounds mad, but that's what happened. The fire came from inside her."

"Thank you. That's all."

The young man stood up. "I don't understand!" he wailed. "How could she just die like that?"

CORONER'S VERDICT: Death by misadventure caused by a fire of unknown origin

On paper—on police, and FBI, and coroners' reports—it is death by fire of unknown origin. But behind closed doors, in whispered conversations, the words are "death by spontaneous human combustion," or SHC for short. It means a sudden, unexplained burning of a human being. Over the years, this terrifying, positively flesh-crawling phenomenon has occurred more times than medical science would care to admit. SHC has claimed at least two hundred known victims. The actual number is probably higher, with the first reported SHC case dating back to 1673.

The ghastly disaster occurs suddenly. It strikes without warning, without any apparent reason, and its advance is so swift, death is inescapable. The fire seems to originate inside the person, with the flames usually bursting out of the victim's torso. The body is consumed within seconds, although sometimes a single limb may be discovered beside the charred remains, strangely unharmed, still clad in a slipper or stocking. In 1966, Dr. J. Irving Bently became a victim of spontaneous human combustion. The body was totally incinerated with one exception. The lower part of the right leg, pink and horribly lifelike, lay among the ashes that had once been Dr. Bently.

Another baffling aspect of SHC is the tremendous heat of the fire. Based on the condition of the victims' remains, the temperature had to have been in excess of 3000° F. The person is literally cremated, and in an extremely short period of time. Witnesses say it all happened too fast for them to do anything. In contrast, the cremation of a corpse takes upwards of three hours.

And then there is the question of why the fire never spreads. Dr. Bently's house should have been an inferno. Any firefighter will tell you how entire blocks of attached houses have been leveled from a single lighted match carelessly tossed into a wastebasket. Why didn't Dr. Bently's house burn? Why weren't the tiles in the bathroom, where the fire occurred, even scorched? Dr. Bently had been using an aluminum walker for a broken hip he had suffered some months earlier. The melting point of aluminum is just over twelve hundred degrees F, yet the walker was found virtually intact right where it had fallen when Dr. Bently let go of it. The walker's rubber tips should have melted like marshmallows, but they, too, were undamaged. Why? How can an SHC fire be so selective when everything in its vicinity is flammable?

Science also cannot find any explanation for a number of other oddities, like Mrs. Reeser's shrunken head, for example. Most people are under the impression that South American headhunters shrink skulls by either drying or heating them. This is not so, and for a very good reason. It won't work. You can't shrink a skull because a skull is bone. Headshrinkers smash the skull and remove the bone fragments through an incision. It's the skin and scalp that are shrunken. So there is no known way Mrs. Reeser's head could have gotten to be as small as it did. It should, in fact, have exploded as the heat, and therefore, the pressure, increased.

It is indeed fortunate that spontaneous human combustion is so rare, because medical science has no clues at all to its cause. Initially, it was suggested that the victims were most likely to be elderly, overweight women who drank too much. The scientists thought that excess body fat combined with alcohol somehow made a person more internally flammable. However, tests have shown that fatty tissue burns rather slowly, and the burn rates for alcohol-soaked and "non alcoholic" tissue are the same. Furthermore, we now know that there is no typical SHC victim. As the list of cases grew, it became apparent that SHC strikes both men and women, regardless of age, weight, body type, or lifestyle.

A more recent theory has blamed the body's phosphorus content as the cause of SHC. Phosphorus is an element that bursts into flames when it is exposed to the air. However, if our phosphorus is the culprit, then we are left with the question of why all of us don't explode.

Yet another theory offers static electricity as a cause. The most common example of this phenomenom is what shampoo manufacturers call "flyaway hair."

Another is the "shock" you get after you've walked across a carpet and touched something metal. Every now and then we all build up a few volts of static electricity, which is then harmlessly discharged through our hair. But some people can build up as much as thirty thousand volts. These "walking live wires" have actually been known to start fires when in the vicinity of flammable materials. If they are the ones who become SHC victims, they provide both the spark and the fuel to keep the fire burning. But that still does not explain why the fire spreads through the body so quickly, how it gets so hot, and why almost nothing else around the person burns.

So where does that leave us?

Well, it leaves us exactly nowhere—without a cause, without an explanation, without even a halfway decent theory. In truth, we know as little about spontaneous human combustion today as the people who discovered the very first victim way back in the seventeenth century. So for the time being, at least, we are forced to stamp this one *Unsolved* and file it under *Bio Amazing*.

CHAPTER 10

A Matter of Life and Death

We come now to the final mystery, the mystery that inevitably faces all of us. In art, it is portrayed as a tall, gaunt man whose face is forever hidden by a black hood and who carries in his pale hand a long, sharp reaper's scythe to harvest the living from the fields of earth.

Death, we are told, is the Grim Reaper, who carries out his duties with solemn swiftness. We can make no appeals, nor can we learn our destination before our time has come. And so, we are both repelled and attracted by this ultimate unknown. We struggle with our mind to probe the mystery of death, to learn what lies beyond all that we know as life, and yet, we run frantically from the Reaper's outstretched arms. We are afraid of the dark because we cannot see what it holds for us.

But perhaps the darkness is not quite so deep. Perhaps for some, a small candle flickers briefly to show the color of the Grim Reaper's bottomless eyes. For in the early morning hours of May 23, 1970, a man who shall be known as Paul Carter came very close to dying in the emergency room of a hospital, and this is his story.

It is just after 1:00 A.M. Paul Carter has spent the evening with a friend and is on his way home. He passes darkened shops... a supermarket, a dry cleaners, a bakery... and his footsteps echo softly through the sleeping streets. Perhaps he slows his pace slightly to release a yawn, but at some point he will step off the curb. Then Fate will play the ace of spades from its hand.

1:12 A.M. A car looms up in the distance, its headlights cutting wide swaths of yellow on the blacktop. Carter hears the engine, the ping of loose gravel against the chassis, but he cannot react. There is no time. The driver catches Carter's shadowy outline and jams the brake with a foot that feels like lead. The wheel spins, the tires squeal, and Carter is slammed from behind. His body bounces crazily across the concrete. Panicked, the driver throws the gears into reverse to find out what he has hit. Carter is run over again, and this time he loses consciousness.

1:23 A.M. The street is clotted with police cars,

their radios crackling static messages. An ambulance pulls up, and Carter's limp body is blanketed and strapped to a wheeled stretcher. The driver of the car peers over a police officer's shoulder at the paramedics. He can't believe what has happened. It seems to be a dream. He wipes the sweat off his upper lip and shuts his eyes.

The emergency room doors bang open, and the ER staff converges upon Carter. Everything is loud and bright, silvery stainless steel, fast and efficient. Carter is still unconscious, oblivious to the pain and noise, hanging onto life with his fingernails.

Suddenly I could see my body in the emergency room. I had been on a gurney, and then they transferred me to a table. I was right there watching, almost like a participant, but further back than anyone else. I had a clear view of everything that was happening, and I kept thinking, "That isn't me," but I knew it was. There were cuts and bruises all over me, and my body was black from the road tar. I wasn't frightened, though. Not in the least. It was all just really strange.

The doctor purses his lips. "I don't know," he mutters. "This doesn't look too good." He points to Carter's bloodied flesh.

I could hear the doctor say I was going to lose my leg. Then I saw them put a tourniquet on me. I remember there was a monitor in back of my head, and all of a sudden the green light going across went flat. One of the nurses said something like . . .

"It stopped! He's in arrest!"

The cardiac monitor is wailing.

"Let's go! Move it!" shouts the doctor. He slams Carter's chest with his fist. Then, fingers linked, elbows locked, he starts the piston push of CPR.

Sounds and movement. The metallic clatter of a crash cart, staccato voices giving orders like machine-gun fire. The doctor's breath coming in gasps. Perspiration. The strange rubbery squeak of rhythmic pressure on a human chest.

"Where are those paddles?"

"On their way, doctor."

They brought out some kind of a machine, and I saw them rubbing these two disc things together.

One of the nurses grabs a plastic bottle from the crash cart and squirts a wide coil of gel on the surface of the paddles. Deftly, he rubs the paddles together, spreading the gel to insure a good contact with Carter's chest.

"Ready." He holds the paddles out for the doctor who is glistening with sweat.

The doctor positions the paddles and glances quickly around. "Everyone clear! And . . . GO!"

Voltage!

I came about nine inches off the table with my back arched. "Oh God!" I thought. "This can't be me!" And then, just like that, I was in total darkness. I started to get scared because I didn't know where I was. I was just sort of floating through this darkness, but then after a little while I could see a light—way, way off, like somebody was holding a flashlight. I started to move toward it, and it got brighter, and brighter, and brighter. It was just so beautiful and peaceful, and even though the light was almost blinding, it didn't hurt at all.

And then there were angels around me, but the angels were my children. They were all the same age— six years old. Even my eldest son, who's seventeen, was six. He was in the lead. Nobody said a word, but as I looked at each of my children, I remembered a very special time the two of us had shared together, a personal private time without the rest of the family.

It was beautiful, so wonderful, and there was an indescribable blue all around me. I've never seen a blue like that. It wasn't like the sky or anything. It was just a . . . a blueness, a brilliant blueness.

Then I felt a slight pressure on my head, and suddenly there was a voice telling me to go back. It was loud and thundering and seemed to be coming out of nowheres. I didn't want to go back and I asked, "Why? Why me?" The voice said my work on earth wasn't over yet. I had to go back and complete it. Go back . . . go back . . . go back . . .

"I'm getting a pulse! BP's coming up!"

The doctor noisily exhales and swipes at his sweating forehead. "God!" he breathes. "I thought we'd lost him."

I don't remember anything after the voice, not until I woke up in intensive care two days later. I'll tell you one thing, though. That place . . . it was so peaceful, just indescribable. If I had my choice, I'd be back there.

Just exactly where was Paul Carter during the moments of his cardiac arrest? To the doctors and nurses who worked to revive him, the question seems ridiculous. "You've got to be kidding!" they'll reply. "He was right here in the emergency room."

But Paul Carter says no. Maybe his body was there, his flesh and blood, but *he* was somewhere else, somewhere beyond the bloodied bandages, and the stink of disinfectant, and the hospital, and perhaps even the very world in which we live. Paul Carter believes he stood at the door to death and glimpsed whatever lies beyond it. He believes that the essence, the mind of Paul Carter was on its way to the next world, and that he would have remained there in eternal peace if only someone or something hadn't sent him back.

Paul Carter had what is called a near-death experience, or NDE. He is not the first. In fact, it is estimated that one out of four people who have a medical crisis similar to Carter's will report an NDE. It will have nothing to do with their religion, their age, their sex, their will to live, or their belief in an afterlife. It will simply occur, and most often coincide with the time that they undergo cardiac arrest—total stoppage of the heart. As medical teams work feverishly to revive them—and revive literally means, "to live again"—these people will feel as though they are beginning some kind of journey, leaving their body behind, and entering another world. They will "return" with vivid memories and a sense of peace and contentment. Each account will be personal and unique, but the same basic elements will appear again and again.

Perhaps the near-death experience is nothing more than a hallucination, a powerful fake created by the brain when it recognizes that death is about to occur. Perhaps it is wishful thinking, or a chemical change caused by drugs, or a dream.

But perhaps it is not.

All of us would like to believe in a hereafter, but you are urged to keep an open mind as you travel through the mysterious phenomenon of the near-death experience. So far, nothing about it has been proved except that it occurs.

Most societies have held the belief that death begins with a journey. The ancient Egyptians buried their pharoahs with small models of papyrus boats to carry the deceased to the next world. When archeologist Howard Carter finally muscled his way into King Tut's tomb, he found the equivalent of a United Van Lines moving truck. Tut had been provided with all kinds of paraphernalia for the trip over. He had food and clothing, weapons in case he met enemies, furniture, the Egyptian version of Monopoly, and other earthly comforts. Obviously, the Egyptians believed in being prepared.

The Greeks and Romans also thought that dying was going to involve long-distance travel. For them, Phase I was a ferry ride across a river that divided life from the heavenly shore. Unfortunately, the ferry pilot demanded prepayment for the cruise, and if you didn't have the money, you would be left behind in a kind of shadowy netherworld, a less than ideal place to spend eternity. So as part of the burial procedure, two coins were placed on the eyes of the deceased for boat fare. This practice became worldwide and is still quite common today.

Those who have had near-death experiences don't mention boats and ferry captains, but they do say they felt as though they were going somewhere. Their first sensation is one of weightlessness, of floating, or as one person phrased it, "like my brain was up in space." They speak of suddenly feeling separated from their body and then slowly, slowly, slowly rising to a great height. It is at this point that about half the people claim to have been able to see their own body—not, mind you, as if they were looking in a mirror, but as if they were an observer standing in another part of the room or hovering overhead somewhere. This bizarre phenomenon is called autoscopy, which comes from the Greek words meaning, "the viewing of one's self."

People who experience autoscopy can see everything with perfect clarity—the faces of anyone turned in "their direction," medical equipment of which they had no prior knowledge but later describe, the furnishings of the room, and even their own physical condition. Paul Carter, if you remember, commented on all the cuts and bruises he had. One young man noticed that his eyes were closed and that he was covered with a hypothermia blanket. Scores of people have heard bits and pieces of conversations, and a few people have reported highly technical remarks made by the surgeon during their own operation.

Oddly enough, none of this seems to upset the NDE person in the slightest. He or she watches even the most drastic resuscitation procedures with cool detachment. Time and again somebody will say, "Sure, I knew it was me down there and that I was dying, but it didn't bother me in the least. In fact, I felt real, real good."

An American soldier in Vietnam, who was profoundly injured in a rocket explosion, saw himself with both legs and an arm blown away. His sense at that time was that he was looking at a mannequin, a dummy. He recalls watching the Viet Cong strip off his boots and rings, and later, somebody putting him in a body bag and loading him onto a truck with the other casualties. He watched all of this without the slightest twinge of emotion.

The soldier says he next saw his body lying on a table in the morgue while preparations were being made to inject the embalming fluid into a vein in his groin. The embalmer made the incision and then suddenly stopped cutting when he noticed that there was a lot of blood. This puzzled him. A corpse has no heart action, so there should be only a trickle of blood. Within minutes it was recognized that the soldier was still alive, and he was immediately rushed into surgery. And that's the last thing the soldier says he remembers until he woke up in the hospital.

Now, will someone kindly explain how any of this is possible? These people who experienced autoscopy were unquestionably "out"—unconscious, or in cardiac arrest, or in deep shock, or under anesthesia. Their eyes were closed. In many cases an oxygen mask obscured their vision. They were facing in the opposite direction, or their head was turned toward the wall. And what about their angle of observation? You have one perspective when you're lying prone and a completely different one when you're standing behind the crowd or high above it, as on a balcony.

But let us suppose that the mind and body are really two separate parts. The body, then, is just a container for the mind, a means of transportation, if you will. When death occurs, the mind is somehow released. It floats upward like a hot air balloon rising from the ground. That would explain how people who have near-death autoscopic experiences are able to see and hear events when their body is no longer functioning.

It should be pointed out, however, that high levels of carbon dioxide in the brain can induce a state similar in some respects to autoscopy. In a carefully controlled study in the 1950s, two hundred people were asked to inhale, by mask, a mixture of thirty percent carbon dioxide and seventy percent oxygen. (Discounting pollution, the air we normally breathe contains only a trace of carbon dioxide.) A large percentage of the subjects in the study said they felt detached from their body, as if they were being pulled upward into space. None, however, were able to describe the events taking place around them or to actually see their body from another point of view.

So, the phenomenon of autoscopy still remains a mystery. But perhaps even more mysterious is the experience that, for many NDE subjects, follows autoscopy.

Interviewer: And then what happened? After you could see your body, I mean.

NDE Subject: I watched for a while and then all of a sudden, everything went black. I was just moving through this blackness. It was like a tunnel, a very dark tunnel.

And so, the next phase of the near-death experience begins. For the first time there is a very real sensation of traveling somewhere, and a lot of people say they knew at this point that they were dying. Some are frightened or apprehensive. "I didn't know where I was going," said one man. "I was a little scared." But in the vast majority of cases the darkness is peaceful and comforting. A woman described it as "space without stars," a great, black void, a nothingness.

On and on they fly, through an intense darkness that could extend a hundred yards, or a hundred million miles, or maybe no distance at all. Dr. Kenneth Ring, a psychologist who has done some research on near-death experiences, believes that this tunnel of darkness may be a link between the world we know and whatever lies beyond. It is a kind of corridor that leads the dying to another level of existence. And at the end, in a somewhere far, far beyond time and space, there is the light.

It appears suddenly, a magnificent radiance that totally envelops the man whose heart has stopped, the teenager who lies unconscious and barely breathing, the woman in profound shock. The light is golden or silver white, intensely bright and blinding, but never uncomfortable or painful. It is brilliant, sometimes a kaleidoscope of pure color, warm, welcoming.

"It was all around me. I had the feeling of total peace. It wasn't the kind of light you get from a lamp. No. ... It was ... it was like ... like someone had put a shade over the sun."

A man said, "Well, it was not a light but the absence of darkness, total and complete."

Another man: "There was this light, like someone holding a flashlight, and I started going towards that. And then the whole thing brightened up, and the next thing I remember was I was floating. I was going through this shaft of light. The light kept getting brighter and brighter. It was so bright, and the closer I got, the brighter it got, and it was blinding."

For some, the near-death experience ends moments

after they see the light. For others, the light is only the beginning.

This may all be a particularly vivid dream, but the people who have had very deep near-death experiences claim to have traveled to a place of extraordinary beauty. In the flash of an instant, they entered the light and found themselves in an environment so wonderous, they struggle miserably in their attempts to describe it. Almost without exception, everybody expresses a desire to return, and they feel certain that when they die, this perfect world will be their final destination. Months, years, even decades later, their memory of it is sharp and clear, the details unaffected by time. What kind of event could possibly have had such an impact?

The place these people saw is one of peace and serenity. It is almost always pastoral—a meadow, rolling hills, fields, a forest.

"I was standing on something high, because down below me there was just the most beautiful, greenest pasture and then just a flat meadow over to my right."

There are streams and rivers with clear blue water, flowers of astonishing color waving gently in soft breezes, tall grass, golden wheat, pine trees, willows.

"I saw the most beautiful lakes .... Everything was white. The most beautiful flowers. Nobody on earth ever saw the beautiful flowers that I saw there. . . . I don't believe there is a color on this earth that wasn't included .... The lakes were blue, light blue."

Some people hear music for which they can find no

earthly comparison. Others describe the soft lowing of cows, horses grazing in the distance, birds, and, most significantly, other people.

"Suddenly I saw my mother who had died about nine years ago . . . she was smiling . . ."

"I was sitting up there somewhere and I could look down. With me was my older brother who had been dead since I was a young feller."

"I came to some place and there were all my relatives, my grandmother, my grandfather, my father, my uncle who had recently committed suicide. They all came towards me and greeted me."

After her experience, one woman reported seeing a man whom she recognized as her grandfather. Even though she had never met him when he was alive, she described him accurately to her grandmother.

Most of the people encountered are deceased relatives, but occasionally, strangers or religious figures are seen. They may be shepherds, people in hooded robes, angels, "heavenly guides," or a man who is taken to be Jesus. Sometimes they come forward to lead the person on or encourage him or her to continue.

"(Then I saw) two aunts of mine—they're dead—and they were sitting on a rail . . . . They started calling to me."

The woman who saw her mother said she heard her speak in Hungarian, her native tongue. "We've been waiting for you. We've been expecting you. Your father's here, and we're going to help you."

The man who met several of his relatives, however,

reported just the opposite. They did not urge him to remain but instead, turned him away. He was told by his grandmother, "We'll see you later but not this time."

This gentle but firm command may also come from a disembodied being—a spirit or presence—that seems to communicate by some sort of telepathy. The person is made to understand that the time for dying is not yet at hand, that he or she cannot remain. Usually, this order is met with resistance. The desire to stay in this wonderful place surrounded by loved ones is overwhelming, and it is here that the person faces a critical decision. Said one woman who saw her dead husband wading across a stream toward her, "If I had gone with him, I would not have come back." This is the turning point, a time to choose, and everyone who reaches it believes it was literally their moment of life or death.

A woman lies recuperating in her hospital bed after touch-and-go surgery. It is a miracle she is alive. Her doctor enters, smiling and jovial, proud of his successful duel with death the night before.

"How are you feeling, Mrs. Archer?" he asks, but he knows the answer.

His patient nods. "Good, but just a little tired."

The doctor sits on the edge of the bed and folds his hands. "You know," he says, "we fought quite a battle in there. I thought we had lost you. No pulse, no respiration. Your heart was at a dead stop. You were gone." He shakes his head at the memory.

"Yes, I know," replies Mrs. Archer. She, too, is remembering. "But I came back. I had a choice and I came back."

Mrs. Archer is recalling the moment of her near-death experience when she believes her future was placed in her own hands. As she stood on a grassy knoll overlooking a gentle meadow with golden wildflowers, she heard a voice. It seemed to come from nowhere and yet everywhere, and it asked her if she wanted to return. Mrs. Archer hesitated. What a beautiful place this was! How peaceful! How glorious! But her children were waiting back on earth, and her husband . . . they needed her . . . she had so much more she wanted to do . . . she couldn't leave now . . .

"I want to go back," she told the voice.

Unlike Paul Carter, Mrs. Archer is a fictitious character, but her experience has been reported by dozens of people who have been near death. At some point, they say, they were either urged to continue their journey or told to return to life. Some maintain they made their own decision; others feel they were sent back.

A salesman whose NDE resulted from an automobile accident said two men "with a terrific sense of humor" and "khaki uniforms" called him by name and said they had been waiting for him.

"We're here to show you the way," they said.

At first, the man accepted his fate and fell into step beside them.

"You know," they continued, "you shouldn't go back. It's too hard for you to go back now."

But the man reconsidered. "No," he said. "I really want to," and the decision was made.

"We don't wish to be abrupt, but we're going to have to be on with it. If you don't wish to go, we've got to be on. But don't be concerned. We'll be back for you."

Another young man apparently had it a little tougher. He claims he had to bargain his way back with a voice he describes as being "soft yet harsh." In his life-and-death debate with the voice, he first points out that his death has come too soon. (He was nineteen at the time.) He says that there are many more things he hasn't done yet. He wants to finish school. Finally, he assures the voice that he will be able to handle all the pain of his recuperation. "So if it's possible," he says, "I'd like to go back."

But some people are not so sure. They feel torn between living and remaining in a place that is wonderful beyond description. Others, like Paul Carter, state flat out that they don't want to leave. So the decision is made for them.

The return trip seems to occur instantaneously, and most people are able to supply very few details. One man said, "This force started drawing me back like a giant magnet. A force stronger than anything we know. I resisted it . . . but there was no way. Then everything went completely black."

"The thing I remember most is a falling feeling. Like I was coming down really fast and then hit. And then I woke up with a jolt."

"It was as though I was seeing many, many lightning and thunderstorms all at once . . . . It was as if I were being pulled out of a tremendous vacuum and just being torn to pieces."

One woman heard, "You're needed, Patricia. I'm sending you back now."

"It was a man's voice," she recalls, "a male voice. And I opened my eyes."

And so it ends, an experience too unbelievable to be real, and yet all too real to be unbelievable.

Science is nervous. It can't ignore the phenomenon, so it struggles to find an explanation. The most popular theory is that these people are hallucinating. The brain, faced with the terrifying truth of its own death, tries to deny it. It produces a host of complex chemicals that create a convincing illusion of peace and beauty. "Don't be afraid," it says to itself. "Nothing will hurt you. You are protected."

But when the people are asked if their NDE was a hallucination, almost everyone insists that it was not. (The remainder aren't sure.) Furthermore, it is really pushing it to suggest that people of different backgrounds, different religions, different ages and lifestyles could have such an incredibly similar hallucination. Although each NDE is unique, not one of them breaks the overall pattern. True, some people experience autoscopy and some don't. Some encounter their deceased relatives and some don't. But absolutely no one, for instance, reports falling into a body of water. The water would be a completely new element, not part of the pattern. In short, everybody keeps to the rules. It's like giving a lot of artists two colors of paint—red and blue. The artists will create an infinite variety of pictures, but they will never paint a picture with green in it.

So if NDE's are not hallucinations, can we then conclude that they're legitimate experiences? Did these people really go somewhere, to an afterworld? Are we seeing evidence of life after death?

Despite the highly detailed, emotional, thoroughly honest stories of these people, we don't have real proof, and for the time being, at least, we are unlikely to get any. During a medical emergency, doctors are far too concerned with saving the patient to start conducting scientific experiments. Even more of a problem is figuring out what on earth we're going to measure with the experiment. If the mind actually leaves the body, how do we catch it in the act? And if we can catch it, is that evidence for life after death? The answer is no. It's only evidence that the mind can leave the body.

In most mystery stories this is where the detective coolly saunters in and brilliantly solves the case. The reader's eyes widen in surprise and sweet satisfaction as the clues fall neatly into place and all is at last made clear. But it won't be that way this time. This time there are no fictional private investigators or clever writers. This time there is only the mystery.

And the mystery is you.

Bibliography

CAUTION: Due to the bizarre nature of the subjects, don't be too quick to accept everything you read as fact. Ask a lot of questions. How reliable are the stories? Who did the research? Are the reports just based on hearsay? Be a reading detective.

To Get You Started

Gadd, Laurence D. *The Second Book of the Strange.* World Almanac Publications, N.Y. 1981, softcover.

> Because this book covers so much, the author couldn't spend a lot of space on any of the subjects. But hang onto your hat because what is there is absolutely fascinating.

Hall, Elizabeth. *Possible Impossibilities.* Houghton Mifflin Company, Boston, 1977.

A journey through the amazing subject of parapsychology. Read with caution, however. Not everything is as baffling as it sounds. A good book to start with, though.

Hyde, Margaret O. *Is the Cat Dreaming Your Dream?* McGraw-Hill Book Company, N.Y., 1980.

Don't let the funny title fool you. This book is serious stuff. A shorty but a goodie. All about dreams and sleep.

————, Edward S. Marks, and James B. Wells. *Mysteries of the Mind.* McGraw-Hill Book Company, N.Y., 1972.

This book has a little of everything. Chapters include: Sleep and Dreams, Hypnosis, and ESP.

Smith, Howard E., Jr. *Dreams in Your Life.* Doubleday & Company, Inc., Garden City, N.Y., 1975.

This book is chock full of all kinds of interesting information, from dream interpretation in various cultures to dream symbolism and facts about sleep itself. There is even a chapter about dreams and ESP.

Bigger and More Challenging

Mysteries of the Unexplained. The Reader's Digest Association, Inc., Pleasantville, N.Y., 1982.

This is not the kind of book you read from front to back. It's a bit like an encyclopedia of the weird, so use the Table of Contents to help you find your way to prophesies and ESP, faith healing, spontaneous human combustion, twins, firewalking, and a lot more.

Sanderson, Ivan T. *Investigating the Unexplained.* Prentice-Hall, Inc., Englewood Cliffs, N.J., 1972.

Sanderson is a wonderful writer and a careful scientist (degrees in zoology, botany, and geology). This book may be a bit tough, but stay with it; it's fascinating. See especially Chapter 15 and Appendix A for spontaneous human combustion.

What and Why It's Missing

Research on near-death experiences has begun only recently, so you may have a tough time finding information about it.

Best Bet: Check the *Reader's Guide to Periodical Literature* for magazine articles.

Spontaneous human combustion will also require some fancy detective work. Most people have never even heard of it! In Charles Dickens' novel *Bleak House* it makes a fictional appearance. Try the *Reader's Guide* for this one, too.

Enjoy!

Index

143